THE
QUEER
ALLIES
BIBLE

THE
QUEER
ALLIES
BIBLE

The Ultimate Guide to Being an Empowering LGBTQIA+ Ally

NV GAY

PUBLISHING
New York, NY

Ig Publishing
Box 2547
New York, NY 10163
www.igpub.com

ISBN: 978-163246-16-98

We need not forget the liberation from suffering that has come before us,
nor dismiss the actions of progress today,
in order to empower the ability for change that has yet to come.

This is dedicated to all of those who have supported me and stood beside me throughout my gender transition, providing me with affirming and unconditional love.

To my wife, my best friend, my rock, my everything.

To my chosen mother, who stepped up to provide me with the love I desperately needed.

To my friends, who have stood beside me through this entire journey.

This book is for you!

CONTENTS

PREFACE

When I was young, I knew I was different—that I was more than the person I was pretending to be. However, I was afraid to show who I really was, for fear that I would lose the love and family connections I had. Therefore, I forced myself to be who I thought others wanted me to be. I secretly explored my true feelings through video games, exploring my gender using avatars and characters with genders different from my own, while always remaining hidden.

As I got older, I became angry, feeling that I had to be "perfect" in my masculinity—the perfect man, husband, teacher, and mentor. This perfection drove me to attempt to take my life multiple times. Eventually I exploded. I couldn't continue. With love and support, I was finally able to receive help. In December 2018, I came out as gender fluid in the middle of a therapy session, and then to my wife later that same day. Since then I have been living as my true self, expressing my gender as I see fit on any given day.

As I have allowed others to see who I really am, some have loved and accepted me, while others have hurt and disowned me. It takes a tremendous amount of strength to step out and let the world see who you truly are. Some will not understand this, and hate you. In the end, losing those kinds of people was beneficial, because I no longer had their hatred in my life. This provided me with the amazing opportunity to choose my family and surround myself with those who love me.

I am often asked what my gender transition journey has been like. I wish I could say that it has been simple and easy. In reality, it has been fraught with many obstacles and challenges— some of my own making, others created by societal norms and expectations. Each of these challenges has provided me with a unique learning experience.

Previously, I was a middle school teacher. However, I left the field of education to become an advocate within the LGBTQIA+ community. Toward this goal, I now work as a Diversity, Equity, and Inclusion (DEI) and LGBTQIA+ inclusion trainer and consultant. I have also been hard at work on an advocacy and awareness campaign through my photography, titled, "This is Trans." This project sets out to change the narrative surrounding the transgender community and the definition of "validity." It was through this project that I found my voice and my passion to be an advocate for the LGBTQIA+ community. Thus stems my call to action in writing this book.

The Queer Allies Bible is a guide and narrative on how to be an affirming ally to the LGBTQIA+ community. Being LGBTQIA+ means having the courage to come out everyday, showing the world your authentic self, without apology. Being queer is nothing to fear, but rather something to celebrate. If you are lucky enough to have experienced the joy of an individual coming out to you, rejoice! This means that you are someone they trust with knowing who they are completely.

While many allies I have talked with all over the world have expressed joy in celebrating their LGBTQIA+ loved one's identity, they have also shared that they are often lost in finding the resources to show them how to be a true ally. I want this book to be that guide, the bible if I may, helping allies turn love and support into action.

The need for this book was brought to my attention at an exhibition of my advocacy gallery, "This is Trans." During an exhibition in Virginia, an older gentleman approached me and asked how he could become a supportive ally to someone in his life who had come out as transgender. He expressed his love for this person, but did not know how to or what steps he needed to follow in order to affirm them in their gender identity. *The Queer Allies Bible* is a comprehensive and easy to digest handbook for those who want to become an affirming and loving ally to the LGBTQIA+ community.

Among the groups that will benefit from the information in this book are educators seeking to create affirming classrooms; businesses that want to create an affirming culture for their employees and clients; healthcare professionals who are looking to establish affirmative policies for their patients; parents who want to be loving allies to their LGBTQIA+ children; and anyone who wants to learn how to become the best ally they can be for their LGBTQIA+ friends, coworkers, and loved ones. No matter how you plan to use this book, you will learn the steps to becoming the ally that LGBTQIA+ individuals truly need.

Please know that your educational journey only begins once you have reached the end of this book. Allyship is something that is bestowed upon you by the LGBTQIA+ community through your continuing affirming actions and support. Learn from others within the community. Learn from those who successfully advocate and empower the community. Learn how to use your unique voice to uplift and empower marginalized voices. Simply put, learn.

Gender identity and sexual orientation are complex topics. There are so many unique identities, and each person has a different interpretation within those definitions. Don't worry if this all seems like a lot—it is! I have to constantly educate myself on various identities and new issues. That is why I wrote this book. I want to create a starting place to help you become a stronger ally to this incredible community.

I guarantee you that there are people in your life who are closeted, fearing that if they were to come out, they would not be accepted. Being an ally to those who are openly out is wonderful, but it is more important to realize that your actions have a great impact on those who are closeted. If you stand up and demand equality in your workplace, school, community, home, and more, those closeted people will notice, and begin to feel like there is a chance for them to live freely. By being an ally, you will save lives!

PART ONE:

INTRODUCTION TO ALLYSHIP

BECOMING AN ALLY

As a human being, it is our responsibility to be respectful to all people, regardless of gender, sex, culture, race, religion, etc.

"How do I become an affirming and loving ally to the LGBTQIA+ community?"

The answer to this question is not simple and will require a lot of work and dedication on your part. A lesson my father taught me that I've held onto throughout my life is that your character is defined by what you do when no one is watching. Allyship can be thought of similarly—you are defined by the small, simple acts you do when you believe no one is looking. An ally is not someone who only acts when there is an audience.

In your quest to become an LGBTQIA+ ally, you first must realize that this is not a title you can bestow upon yourself. Being an ally means taking inclusionary and affirming actions every day to better the lives of LGBTQIA+ individuals. Becoming an ally does not mean you have to become a "liberal" or give up your spirituality. It means putting aside your preconceived notions of how someone should live, and accepting people's beautiful individuality.

There are three main steps to being an LGBTQIA+ ally:

1. **Be Respectful**
2. **Learn**
3. **Advocate**

Understanding these steps and being able to implement them is key. When looking to take action to provide inclusion and affirmations to the LGBTQIA+ people in your life, these three steps work together. You cannot neglect one in favor of others that might be easier for you. Being an ally requires you to work through a lot of uncomfortable situations and over-come many hurdles in order to offer meaningful support to your LGBTQIA+ loved ones, friends, coworkers, and strangers.

1. BE RESPECTFUL

"We deserve to experience love fully, equally, without shame and without compromise." —Elliot Page, American actor

When it comes to being respectful towards LGBTQIA+ individuals, the first point to emphasize is that we are all human, and thus deserve the right to express ourselves as we understand ourselves to be. As the late Supreme Court Justice Sandra Day O'Connor stated, "Society as a whole benefits immeasurably from a climate in which all persons, regardless of race or gender, may have the opportunity to earn respect, responsibility, advancement and remuneration based on ability."[1] Expressing one's gender identity or sexuality does not bring harm to others, whereas suppressing one's self-expression can cause them great harm.

Most LGBTQIA+ individuals have undergone a great deal of struggle in their lives—having to discover who they are while being told that being queer is" wrong" and "sinful." Many have experienced significant pain during their gender or sexual journey, having been cast out of families, losing jobs, being denied access to healthcare, and much more. According to a 2022 Gallup poll, 7.1 percent of Americans identify as a member of the LGBTQIA+ community (0.7 percent identify as transgender).[2] Those numbers are rapidly rising, largely among American youth, with over 20 percent of Generation Z identifying as LGBTQIA+. This means that, more than ever, it is important to understand and respect LGBTQIA+ individuals.

I often hear the argument that respect has to be earned, and that you shouldn't have to respect someone's gender or sexuality unless you choose to. This implies that all people are not born equal, and that they must gain respect through action and merit, not by merely existing. My counter is that respect is not something that should be or needs to be earned. Giving your respect to someone does not mean that you agree with their choices, or who they are as a person—it means that you see them and recognize that their differences do not make them any less worthy or deserving. Respect simply means that you accept that person for who they are. American poet and civil rights activist Audre Lorde wrote that, "It is not our differences that divide us. It is our inability to recognize, accept, and celebrate those differences."

The belief that respect must be "earned" has created a great deal of discrimination against the LGBTQIA+ community. According to the "State of the LGBTQ Community in 2020," a study conducted by the Center for American Progress (CFP), 33 percent of LGBTQ individuals had faced discrimination in the previous year; that number jumped to 60 percent when including transgender individuals. In addition, approximately 30 percent of LGBTQ individuals encountered difficulties in accessing health care due to their identity; 50 percent with transgender individuals.[3] Fifteen percent of LGBTQ individuals claimed to have postponed or avoided medical treatment completely due to harassment or discrimination in healthcare. The staggering amount of discrimination towards LGBTQIA+ individuals directly leads to increased mental health and self harm issues. According the the CFP survey, nearly 52 percent of LGBTQIA+ individuals had recorded issues with their mental health, with nearly 60 percent having attempted suicide.

Our goal as humans should be to coexist, respecting each other's differences. For example, I am a Christian, and even though I do not follow the beliefs of other religions, it is my responsibility to be respectful of their beliefs and practices. I would not force my religious views upon a person whose views were different from my own. The same can be said concerning LGBTQIA+ individuals. While you may not recognize or accept a person's sexuality or gender transition, you should show that individual the respect that all people deserve.

Being a respectful ally begins with experiencing empathy and compassion. One should follow the golden rule: "treat others the same way you want to be treated." This means gracing them with respect, regardless of how different they may be from you. Too often we think only of our situations, believing that our experiences are typical for everyone. Therefore, we struggle to put ourselves in another person's shoes. In order to truly be respectful, we must first recognize someone's needs and understand what we can do to help them.

The need to respect all people is of utmost importance as the LGBTQIA+ community is currently under attack from hate groups that have successfully infiltrated all levels of government, pushing heteronormative and cisnormative mindsets under the disguise of "traditional" Christian family values. Over 500 anti-LGBTQIA+ bills have been proposed over the past five years, with well over 100 passing into law and going into effect.[4] These bills have, among many other things, banned drag performances and transgender-affirming care for adults and youth; forced teachers and professionals to out students; enacted censorship laws; created bathroom bans; and established licenses to lawfully discriminate. It has gotten so bad that some countries, including Canada, have issued travel advisories warning their LGBTQIA+ citizens to avoid traveling to the United States for their own safety.[5]

On a governmental and legal level, one thing that would help counteract the anti-LGBTQIA+ movement would be the passage of the Equality Act. The proposed bill, which has been circulating in Congress in some form since the 1970s, "would amend existing civil rights law—including the Civil Rights Act of 1964, the Fair Housing Act, the Equal Credit Opportunity Act, the Jury Selection and Services Act, and several laws regarding employment with the federal government—to explicitly include sexual orientation and gender identity as protected characteristics."[6] The legislation would also update the 1964 Civil Rights Act "to prohibit discrimination in public spaces and services and federally funded programs on the basis of sex."[7] Presently, LGBTQIA+ people can be denied housing, refused service by businesses citing religious principles, and be denied medical coverage and access to care. While some states have created their own versions of the Equality Act and enacted protections for LGBTQIA+ individuals, nationwide protections are necessary.

While you as an individual do not have the power to pass the Equality Act, you can contact your representatives at the local, state, and federal level and urge them to enact protections for the LGBTQIA+ community.

Laws aside, anyone can do the following in order to be a respectful LGBTQIA+ ally:

Do Not Judge the Way Others Look

You cannot tell someone's gender or sexual identity from their appearance. Many LGBTQIA+ people do not appear "visibly queer," meaning they are not perceived to be LGBTQIA+ by others. That does not diminish their validity. A cisgender man can wear a skirt and heels if he wants to and still identify as a cisgender male, just as a transgender woman can wear a suit and still be valid in their identity.

Don't Buy Into Gender and Sexual Myths

Gender identity does not equal sexual identity, and vice versa. Many people assume that a transgender woman started out life as a gay man and then transitioned into a transgender hetrosexual woman. Dangerous myths of this kind are harmful toward LGBTQIA+ individuals. Simply put, gender and sexuality do not go hand in hand. Sexual orientation is about who we're attracted to; gender identity is about our personal sense of being a man or a woman, or neither of those binary genders. Just because someone identifies their gender in a certain way does not mean that their sexual identity has to match.

Ask, Don't Assume

It is okay to ask someone about their gender identity or sexual orientation—respectfully—rather than making assumptions about who they are. It is always a good idea to ask someone what their pronouns are, and how they would like to be referred to. The best way to do this is by first introducing yourself and sharing your pronouns: "Hi, I'm Alex, and my pronouns are he and him. How would you like me to refer to you?" This is a great way to make a person feel comfortable and let them know that you are an ally they can trust. While many people will claim that this is an unnecessary additional step when meeting someone, think about this: thirty years ago, if you made a phone call, you only needed to dial a seven-digit number for those in your area. Then, in the late 1990s, it became necessary to include the three-digit area code even when making a local call. While it took time to get used to this, eventually most of us stopped thinking about it. Using your pronouns in your introduction is a habit that we are going to have to adopt in order to be respectful towards each other.

At the same time, there are certain things you should never ask someone concerning their gender identity or sexuality. Asking them what their gender is or who they are attracted to is not appropriate, as LGBTQIA+ individuals are very cautious about who they share their identity with, as they have to feel they can trust a person with that information. In addition, never ask a transgender person what their "real name" is. The name a transgender person uses and shares with you is their real name, period. (Transgender people often refer to their "dead name," the name they were given at birth that doesn't align with their gender identity. Their "dead name" is often a painful emotional trigger for them and a huge source of dysphoria.)

Lastly, since it would be inappropriate to ask a cisgender person about the appearance or status of their genitals, it is equally inappropriate to ask a transgender person intimate questions about their body. The only time it is okay is when you have built a relationship with that person and have asked their permission to engage in a personal discussion about their identity.

Always Protect An LGBTQIA+ Person's Confidentiality

If and when an LGBTQIA+ individual shares their gender identity or sexuality with you does not automatically give you permission to share that information with others. LGBTQIA+ individuals are very cautious in choosing who they come out to. If they come out to you, that means they trust you enough to share one of the most important aspects of their life. Do not exploit or break that trust—you do not know who they have come out to already, and who they might still need to come out to in the future.

Respect Their Identity

LGBTQIA+ people use many different terms to describe their experiences. You will find that sometimes, especially with gender, a person will define their identity with a term that is used differently by another person. For example, a person who identifies as "nonbinary" may present themselves as more feminine than another nonbinary person. Both of these people are valid in their identity, as there is no "right" or "wrong" way to present gender or sexual identity. If a person is not sure which term best describes their sexuality or gender, give them time to figure it out for themselves. Don't tell them which term you think they should use. You wouldn't like your identity to be defined by others, so please allow others to define themselves on their own terms.

Be patient with a person who is questioning or exploring their sexual or gender identity, as it may take some time for them to determine what's right for them. They might use a name or pronoun, and then decide to change that name or pronoun. Do your best to be respectful and use the name and pronoun they request. As humans, we all express our understanding of self differently. No identity is more "appropriate" or "correct" than the other.

Understand That There is No "Right" or "Wrong" Way To Transition

This topic has been highly debated, as it was once believed that people who transitioned had to align with the binary understanding of gender. We have discovered, however, that gender is not binary; there are many ways to identify one's gender, and each one is equally valid. Some transgender people's access to medical care, such as hormone replacement therapy and gender-affirming surgeries, is limited, and may affect their ability to align their bodies with their gender identity. Others want their authentic gender identity to be recognized without hormones or surgery. Some transgender people cannot access gender-affirming health care due to a lack of financial resources or access to trained providers. A transgender person's gender identity is not defined by their genitalia or surgical procedures, but by their sense of self.

Avoid Using Words You Believe To Be "Helpful"

While you may intend to be supportive, comments such as the following can be insulting, and damaging to a LGBTIA+ person's mental health:

"I would have never guessed you were transgender. You are so gorgeous/handsome."

"I would date you if you were straight."

"You look just like a real woman."

"Why are all the good ones gay?"

"Why did you choose to be queer?"

"He's so hot. I'd date him even though he's transgender."

"You're so brave."

"You'd pass so much better if you wore less/more make-up, had a better wig, etc."

"Have you considered a voice coach?"

"Trans men/women are hotter than real ones."

"You are totally the top/bottom in the relationship."

"Can I see a before/pre-transition picture of you?"

These types of questions and comments can be very taxing to an LGBTQIA+ person's mental health, as they suggest the person is not presenting their gender identity or sexuality "authentically," or that the person's primary concern is to gain the "approval" of others. While some of these comments may be made with the best of intentions, such as "you're so brave," they can come across as condescending, especially when that person has no other choice than to be "brave" in order to be themselves.

The "I would have never guessed you were trans" comment can be particularly painful. While it sounds affirming, it also dismisses a person's identity. While the goal of some transgender individuals is to "pass" as cisgender, that is not the case for everyone. Think of it like this: a comment such as "you don't look Jewish" is highly offensive because it reflects a stereotypical idea of a "Jewish" appearance. The key is to remember that queer identities are just as diverse as the rest of humanity.

Instead, Use the Following Gender Inclusive Compliments:
"You make my world brighter."
"You are empowering/inspiring"
"You radiate warmth and joy"
"You're energy is contagious"
"I love your style"
"You're confidence is intoxicating"

Never Use Derogatory Terms Such As:
Dyke
Fag or Faggot
Homo or Homosexual
Hermaphrodite
Sodomite
She-male or He-she
Tranny or Transvestite
Sissy
It
Double adapter

These are just some of the many offensive and derogatory terms that have been used to belittle, dehumanize, and discriminate against the LGBTQIA+ community. Yes, sometimes you will hear members of the community use these terms; however, that does not give you the right to use them, too. When in doubt, take the safe route. Use the lived name of a person or their nickname when referring to them. It is never a good idea to refer to someone by their gender, sexual, religious, or racial identity.

Challenge Anti-LGBTQIA+ Remarks or Jokes in All Spaces, Public and Private
LGBTQIA+ people have long been the objects of derisive jokes

and negative comments. Think about how many times "gay" has been used to describe someone in a demeaning way. There are countless examples of this in the media, including on hit television shows such as *How I Met Your Mother* and *The Big Bang Theory*. These "jokes" are not necessary to the plot, and are often just included for a cheap laugh.

For example, in an episode of *How I Met Your Mother*, the main character, Ted, is standing at the altar with Robin, about to get married, when Robin tells him, "I used to be a dude." While this was meant to be humorous, it perpetuates the idea that transgender people are not to be taken seriously. Television writers often include "jokes" mocking transgender womens' gender validity, gay/queer romances, and much more. *The Big Bang Theory* includes many of these types of jokes, which is especially discouraging since the main character, Sheldon Cooper, was portrayed by Jim Parsons, a gay man.

The attitudes presented in these programs are seen as acceptable, and are thus often repeated in general society. This should not go unchecked. If you hear these kinds of comments or jokes, part of allyship is interjecting and explaining that they are not appropriate. Allowing them to continue only encourages others to continue to make these kinds of remarks.

Support A Truly LGBTQIA+ Inclusive Culture

Being an LGBTQIA+ inclusive business or group means truly understanding the needs of the community and implementing policies that help it. It is easier to be inclusive of sexuality, as that does not require a lot of change, since it typically involves people's private lives. Being trans-inclusive is more difficult, as it requires workplaces and communities to make major changes in order to support all gender identities.

One practice is to include your pronouns when introducing yourself, on name tags and in email signatures. These simple acts show those you interact with that they are safe to be themselves with you. When a transgender person sees this, it gives them an increased feeling of comfort and safety.

Set An Inclusive Tone with Your Speech

Use non-gendered language to identify individuals—for example, the "person in the blue shirt," instead of the "woman in the front"; "esteemed guests" rather than "ladies and gentleman." Instead of using "Sir" and "Ma'am," you can use "Mx." (mix) to identify nonbinary people, though even that still represents a gender assumption. The best practice is to remove the honorific altogether. Instead of saying, "How are you doing, sir?" you can say "How are you doing today?" The polite greeting remains, but the gendered language is removed.

Support All-Gender Public Restrooms

Restroom use has become a deeply politicized issue, with lawmakers in many states suggesting that people only use the restroom that matches their assigned sex at birth. This may seem like a simple solution, but it can create tremendous problems. For me, the thought of entering a male restroom while dressed in a feminine way causes great anxiety. Doing this basically outs me to everyone and puts my safety at risk.

Since some transgender, nonbinary, and gender non-conforming people may not feel like they match the signs on the restroom door, we should encourage schools and businesses to have single user, unisex and/or all-gender restroom options. If this is not possible, make it clear that trans, nonbinary, and gender non-conforming people are welcome to use whichever restroom they feel comfortable using. In addition, as an ally, you can offer to accompany a transgender or gender-nonconforming person into the restroom. There is always safety in numbers, and accompanying someone to the restroom can really help put them at ease.

Learn About The LGBTQIA+ Community

Finally, the best way to be respectful towards the LGBTQIA+ community is to simply learn. Check out books, films, YouTube channels, and blogs to find out more about LGBTQIA+ people and the issues they face. I recommend watching the documentaries *Disclosure* and *Will and Harper*. Also, understand that LGBTQIA+ people have existed across cultures and throughout history. What is new is the heightened awareness of gender diversity and the transgender community because of increased media attention in recent years. Seek out resources about how trans people existed in the past, and how the trans community functions in different countries around the world.

Being a respectful ally is an all day, every day mindset. When you begin to pay attention, you will recognize the hatred and discrimination experienced by LGBTQIA+ individuals. It is not your job to fix the discrimination; rather, it is your responsibility to be present and respectful towards these individuals. Allyship is a badge you can proudly wear, but it is one you need to earn everyday. It is okay to make mistakes or slip up from time to time; the key is to acknowledge your mistakes and learn from them. Understand your own limits as an ally, and don't be afraid to admit when you don't know something—it is better to admit ignorance than to make assumptions or say something that may be incorrect or hurtful.

SUMMARY: BE RESPECTFUL

Practice respect by remembering that:

LGBTQIA+ individuals do not have a certain "look."

Gender identity does not equal sexual identity, and vice versa.

Ask someone about their gender identity or sexual orientation, rather than making assumptions about who they are.

It is important to protect an LGBTQIA+ person's confidentiality.

You should listen to the way a LGBTQIA+ person describes their identity.

There is no "right" or "wrong" way to transition.

Best practices for allies include:

Avoiding using backhanded compliments and tips that you may perceive to be "helpful."

Using gender inclusive compliments to affirming LGBTQIA+ individuals.

Challenging anti-LGBTQIA+ remarks or jokes in all spaces, public and private.

Supporting an LGBTQIA+ inclusive culture in your speech and behavior.

Supporting all-gender public restrooms.

Learning about the LGBTQIA+ community.

2. LEARN

While LGBTQIA+ people are becoming more popular in culture and in daily life, they still face severe discrimination, stigma and systemic inequality.

The second step toward being an effective ally is to educate yourself on the issues facing the LGBTQIA+ community.

It is important to understand that it is not the responsibility of LGBTQIA+ individuals to educate you. We are not teachers, and are also under the constant scrutiny of anti-LGBTQIA+ activists who seek to use us as examples of why they should strip away our rights. These activists are looking for any aspect of our appearance or behavior that can be used against us. It is exhausting being in a negative spotlight, and we do not always have the energy or strength to educate our potential allies.

Inform Yourself

Your allyship can begin with a simple Google search. Many LGBTQIA+ organizations such as The Trevor Project and the Human Rights Campaign have comprehensive and easy to understand materials on their websites. Wherever you go to get your information, make sure you are accessing sites that have been written by members of the LGBTQIA+ community. This might require you to do some additional research on the site, but this work will help you receive reliable answers to your questions.

A good place to start your research is by learning about the identities and sexual orientations of the LGBTQIA+ individuals in your life. As mentioned in the previous chapter, there are so many different gender identities and sexual orientations that it can be difficult to learn about them all. Think of it as training for a profession, such as becoming a doctor. Medical practitioners spend years studying the human body and how to treat it, but they are not experts in all fields of medicine. A cardiologist, for instance, has the same general knowledge and skills as most other doctors, but specializes in the heart and is probably not equipped to perform brain surgery.

Learning about the LGBTQIA+ community can be seen in a similar light. While it is important to have a basic knowledge of all gender and sexual identities, familiarize yourself with the identities that are most directly applicable to you. For example, my wife has learned a great deal about the transgender identity experience because I am transgender, but she has only a rudimentary knowledge of what it means to be asexual because no one close to her identifies in that way. You should begin by identifying those identities and sexual orientations that are most significant in your life, and commit to learning as much as you can about them.

Recognize the Challenges

After researching your person's gender identity or sexual orientation, turn your attention to the issues they face. Just reading the news makes it clear how prevalent anti-LGBTQIA+ narratives are in our society, with many politicians pushing extremely dangerous and harmful agendas. Unfortunately, many self-proclaimed "allies" believe that accepting their LGBTQIA+ person is all they need to do. However, being a true LGBTQIA+ ally requires knowing and understanding the challenges and obstacles the community faces, and committing yourself to combating those issuers.

One of the most high-profile areas where the LGBTQIA+ community has been discriminated against is in television and film. To be fair, some progress has been made in the positive depictions of same-sex relationships and transgender identities

THE QUEER ALLIES BIBLE

in recent years. Shows such as *Brooklyn 99*, *Modern Family*, and *Schitt's Creek* have been praised for their authentic queer character development. The short-lived late nineties television show, *Freaks and Geeks*, featured a courageous and inclusive illustration of the intersex community. In the episode, "The Little Things," a character named Amy, the girlfriend of Seth Rogan's character, Ken, was shown as being born with both sets of genitalia. The episode demonstrated the true complexities of someone coming out as intersex to a partner, and the reactions that such courage elicits.

However, this is not the norm. In their 2021 essay, "On *Freaks and Geeks* and Finding My Voice: How Pop Culture Shaped My Poetry," Matt Mitchell (They/Them) wrote that, "[i]ntersexuality, normally, is handled in violent ways by Hollywood. There's the morphodite joke in the 1986 film *Stand By Me*, an equally ableist and transphobic joke in the Netflix's 2018 film *Sierra Burgess Is A Loser*, and everything surrounding the character of Pat is troubling on *Saturday Night Live*. When Jennifer Lawrence's nude photos were published online without her consent, she responded, 'At least I'm not a hermaphrodite.'"[1] As Mitchells explains, the intersex community—along with the LGBTQIA+ community—has frequently been used in film and television as the object of denigrating jokes, or portrayed as inferior to those who adhere to heteronomative/cisnormative cultural expectations.

In addition, shows and movies depicting homosexual men as perverts preying on young boys or men have long been commonplace. Crime programs such as *CSI* and *Law and Order* have often depicted LGBTQIA+ characters as criminals. In adition, transgender characters are not generally played by transgender actors. The most egregious recent case was Eddie Redmayne portraying the famous transgender artist, Lili Elbe, in the film, *The Danish Girl*. In an interview conducted by *The Sunday Times* in 2021, Redmayne conceded that his portrayal of this iconic transgender woman was an error: "I made that film with the best intentions, but I think it was a mistake."[2] By contrast, the 2020 Netflix documentary, *Disclosure*, is a powerful examination of how LGBTQIA+ individuals and the larger community have been impacted by their negative representation in movies and televsion.

Visual media impacts the way we think and react to certain issues. If we constantly see a community portrayed in a hostile light, then as a society we will treat that community in a similar fashion. As allies, we must be vigilant of how our LGBTQIA+ siblings are being portrayed, as it will have an impact on how the general public responds to the community.

While you individually do not have influence over what is being shown on our screens, you do have influence on what people around you are saying, whether in public or on social media. Do not stand idly by and allow someone to spew anti-LGBTQIA+ remarks or jokes. Speak up! Explain why those comments are wrong and how they are damaging. It is difficult to overstate the impact an ally can have simply by standing up for the LGBTQIA+ community. It is only when allies rise up and demand change that change will actually occur—both onscreen and in the real world!

Be Aware of Legislation

Have you ever heard someone say, "I am okay with transgender people as long as they do not go into 'my' bathroom?" The idea that transgender people pose a threat to the public through their bathroom use has led to proposed legislation segregating toilets by gender in local and state governments all over the United States. This sounds strikingly similar to the racial segregation of the Jim Crow era, when public opinion and legislative action created a narrative of "separate but equal," resulting in decades of discrimination against Black people. The 1954 Supreme Court ruling in *Brown v. Board of Education* reversed this doctrine, but now it is returning in the demand for separate facilities for transgender individuals. According to the Trans Legislation Tracker, there have been at least seventy proposed bills targeting transgender bathroom use since 2020.[3] On February 6, 2024, the Republican Governor of Iowa, Kim Reynolds, introduced House Study Bill 649.[4] Writing in *The Guardian*, transgender activist and journalist Erin Reed stated that, "[t]he bill, as drafted, would end legal recognition for transgender people anywhere 'male' and 'female' appear in Iowa code and would require special gender markers for transgender people on birth certificates, measures that were compared to 'pink triangles'' once used to identify LGBTQ+ people by Nazis in the 1940s."[5]

Far worse—the bill seeks to redefine the word "equal." Reed notes that, "[t]he bill states that when it comes to transgender people, the term 'equal' does not mean 'same' or 'identical.'" What, then, does "equal" mean? The bill does not define the word, but declares that in the state of Iowa, "equal" no longer means "same" or "identical" when related to transgender people's rights. The bill not only seeks to redefine "equal," but also ensures that "separate" doesn't mean "not inherently unequal." In short, the bill suggests that members of the LGBTQ+ community are not necessarily deserving of the equal rights promised to all Americans by the Fourteenth Amendment of the US Constitution.

While most current legislation is focused on issues related to gender, some state legislators have begun efforts to overturn *Obergefell v. Hodges*, the Supreme Court case that made same-sex marriage legal in the United States. Religious conservatives argue that marriage is a sacred act between a man and a woman, sanctioned by God. To state that people should not be able to engage in a legal ceremony to express their love and commitment for one another due to their gender or sexuality, is unjust and discriminatory. The United States is not a theocracy; the government is not dictated by a religion, therefore religious beliefs should not influence legislation. Sadly, the proponents of anti-LGBTQIA+ legislation call on their religious beliefs as justification for creating and maintaining discrimination.

It is crucial that we recognize and reject all attempts to legally overturn the hard-won rights of the LGBTQIA+ community. LGBTQIA+ individuals do not need separate bathrooms, dormitories, or any other facilities. In addition, all people deserve the right to marry and live safe and productive lives.

Faith-based Discrimination and "Conversion Therapy"

LGBTQIA+ individuals are no stranger to faith-based persecution, as religious texts and doctrine have long been used to demonize the community for expressing its non-normative gender identity or sexuality.

One of the most harmful and dangerous practices that religious leaders use is "conversion therapy," which is the pseudoscientific practice of attempting to change an individual's sexual orientation, gender identity, or gender expression to align with heterosexual and cisgender norms."[6] The goal of such "therapy" is to use therapeutic sessions and religious texts to "cure" someone of their so-called "sinful" practices and return them to heteronormative culture. According to the Human Rights Campaign,

> Such practices have been rejected by every mainstream medical and mental health organization for decades, but due to continuing discrimination and societal bias against LGBTQ people, some practitioners continue to conduct conversion therapy. Minors are especially vulnerable, and conversion therapy can lead to depression, anxiety, drug use, homelessness, and suicide. To date, California, Colorado, Connecticut, Delaware, Hawaii, Illinois, Maine, Maryland, Massachusetts, Nevada, New Hampshire, New Jersey, New Mexico,

New York, Oregon, Rhode Island, Utah, Virginia, Vermont, Washington, the District of Columbia and Puerto Rico all have laws or regulations protecting youth from this harmful practice. Eight of these state laws or regulations were enacted under Republican Governors. A growing number of municipalities have also enacted similar protections, including at least 70 cities and counties in Arizona, Colorado, Florida, Georgia, Iowa, Kentucky, Michigan, Minnesota, Missouri, New York, Ohio, Pennsylvania, Washington and Wisconsin.[7]

Conversion therapy has been promoted as a means of changing someone's gender or sexual identity based on the idea that LGBTQIA+ identities are a "choice." However, numerous scientific organizations have found these practices to be extremely harmful and have shown that they often lead to self-harm. For example, the American Academy of Child and Adolescent Psychiatry (AACAP)

... finds no evidence to support the application of any 'therapeutic intervention' operating under the premise that a specific sexual orientation, gender identity, and/or gender expression is pathological. Furthermore, based on the scientific evidence, the AACAP asserts that such "conversion therapies" (or other interventions imposed with the intent of promoting a particular sexual orientation and/or gender as a preferred outcome) lack scientific credibility and clinical utility. Additionally, there is evidence that such interventions are harmful. As a result, "conversion therapies" should not be part of any behavioral health treatment of children and adolescents. However, this in no way detracts from the standard of care which requires that clinicians facilitate the developmentally appropriate, open exploration of sexual orientation, gender identity, and/or gender expression, without any predetermined outcome.[8]

The Dangers of Conversion Therapy: Ari's Story

For those LGBTQIA+ individuals who have undergone conversion therapy, the stories are horrific and painful to hear. Ari has given me permission to share her experiences of going through and overcoming conversion therapy.

My name is Ari, and I am a survivor of conversion therapy. As a young child, I knew I was different. Growing up in Appalachia, the church meant everything to my family. Most of my young life was spent going to and being a part of the church. Throughout childhood, I began to discover that my sexuality was different from what it was "supposed" to be. As an Apostolic Pentecostal, I was taught that being gay was a sin, influenced by demons. God had created us in this divine image, yet I knew I was born into the "wrong" body. I knew who I was as a young kid. … I'm asking myself and asking God… why am I this way? Why do I feel this way? And I just remember my family always telling me that being gay was a sin. You would go to hell, you were condemned to hell if you liked the same sex. So I had a battle with believing that God would punish me this way. I did not understand this, as I just wanted to be the person I knew myself to be, the beautiful woman I knew I was. Yet I was constantly made to feel that God was punishing me.

Years of going to camps, attempted conversions, and religious traumas left its marks. Family and church members placing their hands on me, speaking in tongues, and performing exorcism-like rituals upon me, just to cleanse me from these so-called demonic ways.

My sexuality had always been part of who I am, and it wasn't always a choice. I had been sexually abused by a same-sex family member when I was five, which led me to be very sexually active while growing up. Attempts had been made to explain my sexuality due to the abuse, but truly that was not it. The sexual actions themselves did not seem wrong, [for] to me, I was a woman and it felt right. The wrong was the abuse by the family member, and that was never treated.

I sought any way to cope, and that was with drugs. I wanted an escape, I wanted a choice, I wanted a chance to find freedom. I had an uncle who was a partier, and I was jealous because I saw the freedom he had. I wanted to join him, to be high, to leave all of my feelings behind. As a young teenager, I ran away in the attempt to join him and find that freedom I so desperately sought. Unfortunately, this was not the escape I had hoped for. Psychedelic trips from heavy drugs constantly brought up these traumas and sent me into a terrible depressive state, leading to multiple suicide attempts.

Any attempt at recovery was met with unsuccessful and painful conversion therapies performed by family members or the church. They would pray for me and attempt to remove the devil from inside of me. Still, I only felt pain. Years of going through conversion therapy and church camps continuously led me back to drugs as a way to escape from the trauma. It was not until my final suicide attempt, an overdose on pills, did I finally come to a realization: God did make me to be the person I am, and God did not make a mistake. I was given a choice in life, that we are supposed to live our life to the fullest. I don't have to answer to anybody but myself and that's the way I had to live.

At sixteen I once again ran away, but this time I

found an accepting and loving home. Here, I finally found that freedom I had been seeking, the freedom to explore and understand myself. I was given the grace and love to understand my gender identity and sexuality. I was able to discover the woman God truly created me to be, in a healthy and safe way.

Gender transitioning in the 1990s was not easy, and I spent those first years obtaining black market estradiol and taking hormones that were prescribed for others. I faced many obstacles, but what I had finally gained gave me the strength to carry on.

Growing up, having your parents tell you that you are under demonic influence and would go to hell left its scars. It's conflicting, because they were the ones who brought me into this world, and they became my first and worst bullies. To this day, I am still misgendered and deadnamed by them. Yet what they can see is that I am happy.

Life has never been easy for me, but what I have had to overcome has shaped me into who I am today. Remember to never judge a book by its cover. It is easy to dismiss a person as being sinful or wrong because their beliefs or life does not align with what you believe it should be. Understand that we are not all made to be one way. God has placed us on this Earth with free will to live authentically and beautifully as the person we are, not to be judgemental and discriminatory towards others who live differently. I had to overcome the traumas of conversion therapy because those in my life refused to understand that God made me to live as I am. Today, I am proud to proclaim that I am a beautiful transgender woman, and a survivor of conversion therapy.

The Importance of Pride

Pride Month began after police raided the Stonewall Inn, which had been a safe haven for LGBTQIA+ people, and particularly for transgender individuals, in New York's Greenwich Village in June 1969. The Stonewall Inn was owned by the Genovese crime family, who profited from laws that targeted the gay community and forced people to meet in "secret" locations. Police followed the "Three Piece Law" or "Three Article Rule," which stated that individuals could not wear more than two articles of clothing meant for the opposite gender.

Claiming that they were searching for members of the Genovese family, on June 28, 1969, "armed with a warrant, police officers entered the club, roughed up patrons, and, finding bootlegged alcohol, arrested 13 people, including employees and people violating the state's gender-appropriate clothing statute (female officers would take suspected cross-dressing patrons into the bathroom to check their sex)." [9] As the police conducted the raid, the patrons gathered outside and began to resist. As people were being led away in handcuffs, objects were thrown at the police.

As news of the riot spread, protests began to pop up in cities all across the country, demanding equality for the gay and lesbian community. A year later, a nationwide protest was begun, calling for queer rights. However, it was not until 1999 that President Bill Clinton declared June to be officially recognized as Pride Month. Today we celebrate the month with parades and festivals, as well as honoring the trailblazing leaders who fought so hard to create a world where LGBTQIA+ people have the opportunity to thrive.

Learn About the History of HIV / AIDS

According to HIV.gov, "HIV (Human Immunodeficiency Virus) is a virus that attacks cells that help the body fight infection, making a person more vulnerable to other infections and diseases. It is spread by contact with the blood or semen of a person infected with HIV, most commonly during unprotected sex (sex without a condom or without the protections offered by medications designed to prevent or treat HIV), or through sharing injection drug equipment. If left untreated, HIV may develop into AIDS, or Acquired Immuno-Deficiency Syndrome."[10]

It is important to state that HIV is not a "gay disease." Without the proper precautions, anyone can contract HIV and spread it. The disease was first diagnosed in the United States in the late 1970s, yet it was not brought to the attention of the public until the early 1980s. Why did it take so long? Unfortunately, early cases of HIV-infection primarily in gay men led to the belief that the condition was a disease of the gay community only. Public attitudes toward the LGBTQIA+ community were generally negative back then, so "[i]t didn't take long for fear of the 'gay plague' to spread quickly among the gay community. Beyond the mortal danger from the disease, they also dealt with potentially being 'outed' as homosexual if they had AIDS or an illness resembling it."[11]

In those early years, government funding for HIV/ AIDS research was inadequate, leading to the deaths of thousands of people. Finally, in September 1985, in response to a question from a reporter, President Reagan finally mentioned AIDS publicly, calling it a "top priority" for his administration. A few months later, Congress allocated nearly $190 million for research and Reagan appointed a commission to investigate the epidemic. In 1987, AIDS Awareness Month was launched.[12]

One case in particular that was instrumental in changing the public perception of HIV/AIDS was that of Ryan White. Ryan was a thirteen-year old boy living in Indiana who had been born with hemophilia, a rare disorder in which the blood does not clot properly. Upon receiving a transfusion in December 1984, Ryan contracted AIDS. At the time, public awareness and education about the disease was low; misinformation and fear were widespread. Ryan faced AIDS-related discrimination, including having to fight to be able to attend public school.[13]

Though he was initially given just six months to live, Ryan survived for five years after his AIDS diagnosis. His death in 1990 led to a shift in attitudes about HIV/AIDS prevention and treatment.

While HIV/AIDS was once seen as a death sentence, recent advances in treatment have rendered the disease highly manageable, lowering incidents of transmission and allowing many HIV-positive individuals to live long and productive lives.

In early 2023, the Centers for Disease Control (CDC) and Food and Drug Administration (FDA) began to loosen the restrictions around gay and bisexual men donating blood. In the past, fear that gay and bisexual men might unknowingly contaminate the blood supply with HIV led authorities to insist that they abstain from having sex for ninety days before donating. The updated guidelines allow gay and bisexual men who are in a monogamous relationship to donate blood. On August 7, 2023, the American Red Cross implemented the FDA's updated final guidance regarding an individual donor assessment for all blood donors regardless of gender or sexual orientation, eliminating previous FDA eligibility criteria based on sexual orientation.[14]

Despite these scientific and medical advances, thirty-four states still have laws on the books that criminalize behaviors that were once believed to lead to HIV infection. According to the CDC,

> During the early years of the HIV epidemic, many states implemented HIV-specific criminal exposure laws to discourage behavior that might lead to transmission, promote safer sex practices, and, in some cases, receive funds to support HIV prevention activities. These laws were passed at a time when very little was known about HIV, including how HIV was transmitted and how best

to treat the virus. Many of these state laws criminalize behaviors that cannot transmit HIV—such as biting or spitting—and apply regardless of actual transmission, or intent. After over 30 years of HIV research and significant biomedical advancements to treat and prevent HIV transmission, many state laws are now outdated and do not reflect our current understanding of HIV.[15]

One such case was that of twenty-three-year old Caymir Weaver, who faced a felonious assault charge and up to eight years in prison for not notifying his partner of his HIV status. Caymir, who identifies as male but was assigned a female identity at birth, was sentenced to serve one year at the Ohio Reformatory for Women in Marysville. At the sentencing, Judge R. Scott Krichbaum reportedly told Caymir, "[y]ou disrespect everything that's proper and moral and ethical."[16]

Laws that punish people infected with HIV worsen the stigma surrounding HIV and AIDS, and discourage LGBTQIA+ individuals from getting tested. The CDC recommends that "[t]alking openly about HIV can help normalize the subject. It also provides opportunities to correct misconceptions and help others learn more about HIV."[17]

Homelessness

According to the National Alliance to End Homelessness, in 2022 over half a million people across America were actively experiencing homelessness. And while some 10 percent of youth in this country identify as LGBTQIA+, among homeless youth, over 40 percent identify as LGBTQIA+.[18] A quarter of homeless LGBTQIA+ young people report that they were kicked out of their family home solely because of their gender identity or sexual orientation. The National Coalition for the

Homeless (NCH) reports that, "[h]omeless LGBTQ youth are more likely than their straight counterparts to engage in survival sex (the exchange of sexual favors for basic needs, like food, clothing, and shelter), with a Canadian study finding that transgender youth are 3 times more likely to engage in survival sex than cisgendered youth."[19]

Many LGBTQIA+ youth are harassed or abused in homeless shelters, causing them to avoid shelters altogether. This puts them at risk for violence, trafficking, disease, and self-harm. The NCH offers the following advocacy responses to LGBTQIA+ homelessness:

> Since a main cause of LGBTQIA+ youth homelessness is family rejection, efforts should be undertaken to either prevent youth from being thrown out of the homes, or to reunify families and open the minds of parents whose children are already homeless.
>
> Demand that federal, state, and local agencies ensure that LGBTQIA+ youth are placed in safe and affirming foster homes.
>
> Place transgender youth and adults in safe and appropriate shelter and housing programs based upon both their gender identity and an individualized assessment.
>
> Schools should be a safe haven for all youth, including those who identify as LGBTQIA+. We need to address the role unsafe schools have in promoting youth homelessness, and aggressively counter school bullying. We also should better ensure that homeless youth are able to continue their education.
>
> Shelter staff, foster parents, and agencies need to be trained on how to be allies to LGBTQIA+ individuals, with written policies to ensure that discrimination does not occur.

Dedicated shelters for LGBTQIA+ people and youth are needed! In addition, it is beneficial for LGBTQIA+ individuals who are experiencing homelessness to see LGBTQIA+ staff working at shelters, since they can provide unique understanding and inspiration.[20]

The Criminalization of LGBTQIA+ Lives

More than sixty nations currently have legislation on the books that target LGBTQIA+ individuals. Many of these countries use anti-sodomy laws against male same-sex activity, and laws against "lesbianism," to criminalize female same-sex activity. Several countries also criminalize being transgender.[21] The ten most dangerous countries for LGBTQIA+ individuals in 2023 were: Libya, Sudan, Malaysia, United Arab Emirates, Guyana, Malawi, Kuwait, Nigeria, Saudi Arabia and Brunei, while the ten "safest" were Canada, Sweden, the Netherlands, Malta, Norway, Portugal, Spain, Denmark, Belgium, and the United Kingdom.[22]

That the United States was twenty-fifth on the list—and falling—is not a surprise. Between 2020 and 2023 over 1,500 anti-LGBTQIA+ bills were proposed in this country (compared to 175 between 2015 and 2019).[23] As we have seen, a growing number of states have enacted bans on gender-affirming healthcare for minors. And of course, bathroom bans are all the rage. Proponents of these bans claim they are protecting women and children from male predators. Kelly Kohls, from the National School Boards Leadership Council and Moms for America, responded to the fact that many college students choose to live on all-gender floors in college dorms by saying, "I would think students would have been traumatized by having to share these spaces. Women need to understand that they walk this earth as prey."[24]

A transgender child using a restroom aligning to their gender does not put other children at risk. Instead, forcing transgender individuals to use a bathroom that aligns with their assigned sex at birth actually increases their chance for harm. Mary Lightbody, a Democratic State Representative from Ohio, said that, "[a]t the college level, transgender college students are victims of sexual assault at approximately the same rates as cisgender students. Do you know who the perpetrators of these attacks are? One-hundred percent of them are cisgender men. The issue here is more about the attacking of women rather than focusing on the behavior of [transgender] students."[25] The group Advocates for Trans Equality states that, "[t]ransgender-inclusive policies do allow for men's and women's rooms, and do not require gender-neutral bathrooms. Instead, transgender-inclusive policies allow all people—including transgender people—to use the bathroom that best matches their gender identity. Those who are living as women use the women's room, and those that are living as men use the men's restroom."[26]

In May 2022, a bathroom ban was passed in Oklahoma mandating that students from pre-kindergarten through twelfth grade use the bathroom that aligned with the sex listed on their birth certificate. Many opposed this law, stating that it would lead to unsafe conditions for transgender and nonbinary students. This concern became a reality in February 2024 when a sixteen-year old nonbinary student, Nex Benedict, died after being attacked in a female bathroom at Owasso High School. The bullying against Nex reportedly began in 2023, shortly after the Oklahoma bathroom ban was enacted, and escalated to physical violence. A cisgender female student struck Nex, resulting in head injuries that sent them to a hospital. Nex died by suicide the following day.

Gender-Affirming Healthcare
Politicians across the United States have sought to remove access to gender-affirming health care for LGBTQIA+ individuals. Oklahoma SB 129 seeks to make it illegal for individuals under the age of twenty-six to receive gender-affirming care

and threatens medical professionals who seek to assist these individuals.[27] While this bill has not passed in Oklahoma, similar bills have been proposed and passed in other states. Florida Senate Bill 245, which passed on May 18, 2023, states that,

> Granting courts of this state temporary emergency jurisdiction over a child present in this state if the child has been subjected to or is threatened with being subjected to sex-reassignment prescriptions or procedures; providing that, for purposes of warrants to take physical custody of a child in certain child custody enforcement proceedings, serious physical harm to the child includes, but is not limited to, being subjected to sex-reassignment prescriptions or procedures; prohibiting certain public entities from expending state funds for the provision of sex-reassignment prescriptions or procedures; prohibiting sex-reassignment prescriptions and procedures for patients younger than 18 years of age; requiring the department to immediately suspend the license of a health care practitioner who is arrested for committing or attempting, soliciting, or conspiring to commit specified violations related to sex-reassignment prescriptions or procedures for a patient younger than 18 years of age, etc. [28]

It will take a concerted effort by LGBTQIA+ individuals and their allies to defeat such legislation and protect patients and practitioners alike. We must call legislators, send emails or letters, provide testimony in opposition to these bills, and attend rallies, town halls, and demonstrations. We are stronger when we are united.

The "Gay Panic" Defense

The LGBTQ+ Bar, a national organization of legal practitioners dedicated to LGBTQIA+ equity, describes the "gay panic defense" as

> ...a legal strategy wherein defendants charged with violent crimes weaponize their victim's real or perceived sexual orientation or gender identity/expression to reduce or evade criminal liability. It is not a freestanding defense to criminal liability. Rather, the defense is a legal tactic that bolsters other defenses, such as insanity, provocation, or self-defense. When a defendant uses the LGBTQ+ 'panic' defense, they argue that their violent actions are both explained and excused by their victim's real or perceived sexual orientation or gender identity/ expression. The goal of this strategy is to employ homophobia and transphobia to persuade a jury into fully or partially acquitting the defendant. Whether or not this appeal to bigotry is successful in court, every time a defendant invokes the LGBTQ+ "panic" defense, they reinforce the dangerous and discredited belief that LGBTQ+ lives are worth less than others.[29]

One of the most recognized uses of the "panic" defense was in the 1988 case of twenty-one-year old Matthew Shepard, who was brutally beaten by two men, tied to a fence, and left to die outside Laramie, Wyoming. Attorneys for the accused killers used the "gay panic" defense in an attempt to justify the actions of their clients: "During opening statements, the defense told jurors that the crime was triggered by a combination of McKinney's drug and alcohol use, traumatic youthful homosexual episodes and an unwanted sexual advance by Shepard."[30]

Shepard's killers were found guilty of his murder, but the tactic has been used successfully in other cases. This defense seeks to excuse violent actions towards a marginalized individual rather than addressing the possibility that underlying homophobia, transphobia, or racism motivated the crime. It has been used to acquit people of their crimes, as with Daniel Spencer's fatal stabbing by his neighbor, Robert Miller, in Austin, Texas in 2018. According to NBC News,

> In 2015, Spencer invited Miller to his house for a night of music and drinking. According to Miller's attorney, Charlie Baird, the men had only met twice before and bonded over their love for music. Miller claimed that he rejected a kiss from Spencer, his attorney said, which allegedly provoked the younger and larger man to fly into a rage. Miller then alleged that Spencer lunged toward him and threatened him with a glass, prompting Miller to defend himself by stabbing Spencer with a knife, according to Baird.[31]

In this case the defense successfully employed the "gay panic" defense by claiming that Miller stabbed Spencer while defending himself from an unwanted sexual advance: "A jury recommended that the defendant, Robert Miller, 69, receive 10 years probation for killing his neighbor, 32-year-old Daniel Spencer. The judge added the maximum six months jail time, required Miller to complete 100 hours of community service, and made Miller pay almost $11,000 in restitution to Spencer's family."[32]

Currently, nineteen states, as well as Washington DC, prohibit the use of the "gay panic" defense, with Delaware and Michigan becoming the latest, in October 2023.[33]

The Sum of All Things

Equality is not a pie where rights are broken up as pieces and then split between communities. If rights are granted to one group, they should not be taken from another. At present, forty-nine states have seen legislation that threatens the LGBTQIA+

community's right to self-expression, health care, and personal safety. Many elected leaders support the exclusion of LGBTQIA+ individuals as part of a narrative of "nationalism" and "traditional Christian family values." As long as we continue to see anti-LGBTQIA+ legislation proposed and passed, violence and hate crimes directed at the community will continue to occur. LGBTQIA+ people are entitled to a life where they are able to live authentically, without fear and discrimination, just as every human being deserves.

Summary: Learn

To become an effective ally:

Inform yourself about the challenges faced by the LGBTQIA+ community.

Be aware of legislation that has a positive or negative impact on the community.

Work to dismantle the dangerous practice of "conversion therapy."

Support Pride events in your area.

Educate yourself and others about the realities of HIV/AIDS.

Understand why many LGBTQIA+ youth experience homelessness.

Join the fight to preserve and protect the community's right to health care.

Argue against all instances of the "gay panic" defense.

3. LGBTQIA+ Around the World

We have existed all over the world and will continue to exist and thrive!

Equaldex (https://www.equaldex.com), a knowledge base that tracks LGBTQIA+ rights across the globe, ranks individual countries on two main criteria—legislation and public opinion. The legislative part of their Equality Index measures "thirteen different issues ranging from the legal status of homosexuality, same-sex marriage, transgender rights, LGBT discrimination protections, LGBT censorship laws, and more," while the public opinion component "measures the public attitudes towards LGBT people using surveys and polls from reputable organizations."[1] Currently, the top ten countries for LGBTQIA+ equality are Iceland, Norway, Denmark, Malta, Uruguay, Canada, Andorra, Spain, and Chile. (The United States ranks twenty-sixth.)

Each of the top countries on the Equality Index has legalized same sex marriage as well as gender transition, with or without surgery. Transitioning genders is not simple, nor does it follow a standard process. Some people choose to only transition socially, some require hormone therapy, while others might need surgical procedures. Therefore, protecting gender-affirming care on a national basis is critically important. In the United States, health care can vary from state to state, with some states seeking to remove a person's ability to transition altogether.

The majority of the top ten countries on the Equality Index also legally recognize a nonbinary gender, allowing gender markers such as "x" on official identifications, as well as banning the practice of conversion therapy. Most have also enacted constitutional protections against housing and employment discrimination for LGBTQIA+ individuals.

The Weight of Public Opinion

While legal protections are critically important, legislation is often driven by public opinion. Many politicians, media members, and celebrities use their positions to offer support or, in some cases, to discriminate against the LGBTQIA+ community. This is not unique to the United States. Other nations, including the United Kingdom and France, support same-sex equality, especially in marriage and adoption, but have been slower to accept and support legal protections for transgender individuals. How the public views the LGBTQIA+ community is directly related to how safe individual members feel in that country.

In December 2023, I had the opportunity to visit Iceland, the number one country on the Equality Index, and experience its friendly, affirming attitudes. As I traveled the country, getting to know its people, I was treated with the utmost dignity. My name and pronouns were always respected, and my wife and I never experienced hostility related to our lesbian relationship. (By contrast, my wife and I have had difficulties while traveling in the United States, with people making inappropriate comments or creating uncomfortable situations for us.) Even the Evangelical Lutheran Church of Iceland recognizes, accepts, and affirms the LGBTQIA+ community, allowing anyone to participate in its services, and permitting all marriages. They even have roads painted with rainbows that lead directly to the church. The church is not trying to make a political statement by displaying rainbows or promoting inclusion; rather, it is signaling that all are welcome and loved. It is simple actions of inclusion and acceptance that have made Iceland the top country for the LGBTQIA+ community.

For LGBTQIA+ individuals, knowing how a country ranks in its equality score is crucial, as we have to weigh our travel options according to how safe we will be. I will not travel to several countries solely for the reason that I am likely to be discriminated against or even subjected to criminal persecution. Several popular travel destinations in the Caribbean, including Jamaica, Dominica, Grenada, Guyana, St. Lucia, St. Vincent, and the Grenadines are unsafe for LGBTQIA+ individuals.[2] These countries all have extremely low scores on the Equality Index, and also have laws criminalizing LGBTQIA+ relationships, as well as extremely negative public attitudes towards the LGBTQIA+ community as a whole. While LGBTQIA+ individuals are typically safe inside resorts in these countries, they can be subjected to discrimination when traveling outside. Though the anti-LGBTQIA+ laws in these countries are seldom enforced, they still provide "social and legal sanction for discrimination, violence, stigma, and prejudice against lesbian, gay, bisexual, and transgender individuals."[3]

Discrimination in the Name of Religion

The countries that rank low on the Equality Index generally have one thing in common—religious persecution towards the LGBTQIA+ community. While the countries within the bottom half of the Index represent a range of religious practices, they uniformly use religious beliefs to justify discrimination against and persecution of individuals for same-sex relationships or gender transitioning.

Religion should celebrate diversity and promote inclusion. In 2023, Pope Francis approved the blessing of same-sex marriages, but insisted that these marriages could not be performed within the church, or by the clergy. The Associated Press noted that "while the Vatican statement was heralded by some as a step toward breaking down discrimination in the Catholic Church, some LGBTQ+ advocates warned [that] it underscored the church's idea that gay couples remain inferior to heterosexual partnerships."[4]

Many activists in the LGBTQIA+ community feel that the blessing of same-sex marriages is not the equivalent of recognizing and affirming same-sex marriage. Ben Huelskamp, executive director of LOVEBoldly, says that, "rather than talking about this in terms of getting married, this is like if a priest was to bless two people on their 50th wedding anniversary...It really doesn't convey anything marriage-wise. It has no ecclesiastical standing for marriage."[5] While increasing numbers of religious institutions have shifted to a more accepting position, far too many continue to actively work against the LGBTQIA+ community.

The influence of religion on public attitudes reaches far beyond the church. In 2023, the National Hockey League (NHL) ended its "Hockey is for Everyone" initiative after seven players chose to not wear special warm-up uniforms designed to promote gender-inclusion by claiming that "inclusion" violated their religious beliefs. This decision by the NHL showcased the damage that is done by removing inclusionary and diversity practices and initiatives. I particularly found the words of Frederik Frandsen to be powerful, in an article he wrote for Last Word on Sports:

> The purpose of these events was never to show that the players were coming out or being part of the LGBTQ+. A fact that some players unfortunately hinted at being a reason they refused to wear the jersey last season. Nobody wants a player to be something they aren't. They should be themselves, just like members of the LGBTQ+ community have a right to be themselves. All wearing a rainbow jersey or tape really shows is that they support those who are part of the LGBTQ+ community. It shows them the right to be themselves. Nothing more and nothing less. That support is what the NHL banned tonight. The right to show appreciation to a group of fans, who unfortunately in some instances won't receive

it in their daily lives. A gesture the NHL has spat on and ruined for many hockey fans, who rightfully should feel betrayed by the league as the NHL's official stance now is that the LGBTQ+ fans are not accepted or respected by the sport for being gay, bi, trans or any part of the LGBTQ+. A truly despicable and evil stance that will tarnish all the goodwill the NHL had gained prior to last year.[6]

Hockey is globally popular, and involves athletes from all over the world. The NHL's decision to end the "Hockey is for Everyone" initiative illustrates the negative influence religion can play—even in international sports.

Progress in the Struggle for Equality

While there is a lot of negativity towards the LGBTQIA+ community around the world, there has recently been some positive movement. Moldova, the Netherlands, Bulgaria, Antigua, and Barbuda all passed legislation banning discrimination against LGBTQIA+ individuals. Norway, Finland, Switzerland, the United States, and parts of Australia have loosened restrictions on blood donation by homosexual and bisexual men. Additionally, several countries, including Namibia, Mauritius, Barbados, and Singapore have decriminalized same-sex marriage, while Estonia, Andorra, and Switzerland have passed legislation granting full marriage equality.

According to Equaldex, 132 nations no longer consider homosexuality a crime, though same-sex marriage is legal in only 35 countries. Seventy-eight countries recognize gender transition, although forty require surgery in order for the transition to be legally recognized. At present, only thirteen countries legally recognize third or nonbinary genders. While these numbers might seem low, Equaldex reports an upward trajectory as more countries move to legalizing LGBTQIA+ rights.

What Can You Do?

While you may not be able to directly influence international public opinion and legislation, as an ally you can research the rights for LGBTQIA+ individuals around the world in order to support your loved ones when they travel. Be aware that some places are not safe for LGBTQIA+ people, as traveling in hostile areas is emotionally taxing and, in some instances, physically dangerous. As an ally, be prepared to advocate on behalf of your LGBTQIA+ companions if necessary, and if you are traveling with them, provide your unquestioning support if they feel threatened or uncomfortable.

While it is unlikely that LGBTQIA+ people will face criminal prosecution while traveling in most Western European countries, they may face other forms of subtle discrimination. This discrimination often occurs in ways that a hetrosexual/cisgender person may not recognize, such as attitudes from strangers in public spaces, unfriendly service in restaurants or accommodations, or complications if an LGBTQIA+ seeks medical treatment. It is important to research the region you plan to visit and to avoid places where reports of homophobic acts have occurred. Equaldex offers information on both domestic and international locations. Other websites, such as *Travel and Leisure*, The International LGBTQ+ Travel Association, and The Queer Travel, may also prove useful. Taking the time to plan your trip carefully will ensure the best possible outcome for everyone.

Summary: LGBTQIA+ Around the World

Attitudes toward the LGBTQIA+ community vary widely between different countries, adding to the complexity of the struggle for gender equality. This chapter focused on:

International Attitudes About Legal Same-Sex Marriage and Gender-Affirming Heathcare

The Weight of Public Opinion

Discrimination in the Name of Religion

Progress in the Struggle for Equality

4. Understanding and Supporting Gender Transitioning

"Being transgender is not just a medical transition. … [It's about] discovering who you are, living your life authentically, loving yourself, and spreading that love towards other people and accepting one another."—Jazz Jennings, LGBTQ rights activist

The concept of "gender" is not determined by a person's genetic makeup or which sexual organs they possess, but is actually a highly personalized form of self expression and self-presentation. It is not as simple as the binary concepts of "male" or "female," but is tied to an individual's self-understanding and how they choose to share themself with the world. It is dehumanizing to identify a person solely by their sexual organs, and the male/female binary of gender identity is not only restrictive, but it excludes intersex people who are born with multiple sex-specific organs.

While all people share certain genetic traits, individuals define themselves in personal ways. Should their gender determine the way they are treated? Does their ability to express themselves diminish their value as a person? No! The idea that every person's gender identity should be "fixed" and defined by social tradition is tied to the misogynistic assumption that males should dominate others. Traditional concepts of "masculinity" are challenged by LGBTQIA+ individuals, whose sexual and gender identities do not adhere to binary constructions of gender, and call for a rethinking of male authority.

The Transgender Umbrella

"Transgender" is an adjective used to describe a person whose gender identity is different from the sex they were assigned at birth. Transgender people have existed throughout history and in every culture on earth. The first step to understanding and supporting gender transitioning is to realize that this is nothing new. Over the centuries, transgender people have lived authentic and successful lives. While the term "transgender" was not coined until the 1960's, transgender people are known to have lived openly in many societies as early as 5000 to 3000 BCE. In ancient cultures, transgender people were often seen as god-like figures and served as priests and healers. The first record of gender reassignment surgery being performed was in Germany in 1931.

The myth associated with being transgender is that a "typical" process occurs as a person transitions from the gender they were assigned at birth to their "true" gender. Another myth is that, as with the popular transgender icon Dylan Mulvaney, many people use their gender transition as a means of becoming famous. This is far from the truth. Transgender people do not transition for any reason other than their need to survive.

The terms "gender spectrum" and "umbrella," have grown in recent years as many different and unique gender identities have gained understanding and validation. Each person is unique and may understand their gender identity differently, even if they choose to describe themself with commonly used terms. The best way to understand how someone identifies their gender is to ask that person and then use the terms they prefer when referring to themselves.

This list defines some of the various transgender identities commonly used both in the United States and in other cultures.

Agender: Someone who doesn't identify with the idea or experience of having a gender.

Androgyne: A person with a gender that is both

masculine and feminine or in between masculine and feminine.

Aporagender: An umbrella term and nonbinary gender identity describing the experience of having a specific gender that's different from man, woman, or any combination of the two.

Autigender: A term that some autistic people use to describe their relationship with gender. Specifically, it means that they feel that their autism affects the way they perceive and feel about gender.

Bakla: Refers to a Filipino person who possesses male sexual characteristics but identifies with femininity and often expresses their gender through feminine dress and behavior.

Bissu: Refers to a person of the Bugis ethnic group of South Sulawesi, Indonesia, who embodies the totality of masculinity and femininity.

Calabai: Refers to a person of the Bugis ethnic group who have male sexual characteristics but occupies a role traditionally occupied by women.

Calalai: A person of the Bugis ethnic group who have female sexual characteristics but present in traditionally masculine ways.

Demigender: This umbrella term typically includes nonbinary gender identities and uses the prefix "demi-" to indicate the experience of having a partial identification or connection to a particular gender.

Demitrans: This nonbinary gender identity describes someone who identifies partially, but not completely, as transgender due to being partly their assigned gender at birth and partially something else.

Demiboy: This nonbinary gender identity describes someone who partially identifies with being a boy, man, or masculine.

Demigirl: This nonbinary gender identity describes someone who partially identifies with being a girl, woman, womxn, or feminine.

Demienby: This gender identity describes someone who partially identifies as nonbinary.

Genderfluid: The experience of moving between genders or having a gender that changes over a period of time.

Genderqueer: Someone with a gender that can't be categorized as exclusively male or woman, or exclusively masculine or feminine.

Graygender: Someone who experiences ambivalence about their gender identity or expression, and doesn't fully identify with a binary gender that's exclusively man or woman.

Hijra: Culturally connected to South Asia and India in particular, Hijras are people who are assigned male at birth but who have woman-identified gender identity and expression. For more than 4,000 years, Hijras have lived in well-structured communities. Since the 1900's, they have created a social justice movement in an effort to be seen in a third gender category, as opposed to either male or female.

Intergender: Someone who's experience of having a gender falls somewhere in between woman and man, or is a mix of both man and woman.

Intersex: A person with a lesser combination of

hormones, chromosomes, and/or anatomy that are used to assign sex at birth. There are many different ways to be intersex, including conditions such as Klinefelter Syndrome, Androgen Insensitivity Syndrome, and Congenital Adrenal Hyperplasia. Some intersex individuals identify as transgender, and some do not. This is determined by the individual person and how they were assigned their gender at birth. Some intersex individuals do align with the gender they were assigned at birth (male or female) while others feel that their gender does not align with the one assigned at birth.

Maverique: Someone who experiences gender or has a core gender identity that is independent of existing categories and definitions of gender, man or woman, masculine or feminine, and androgynous or neutral.

Multigender: A person who experiences more than one gender identity.

> *Bigender*: Identifies with two distinct genders.

> *Trigender*: The experience of having three gender identities, simultaneously or over time.

> *Pangender*: Someone who experiences all or many gender identities on the gender spectrum simultneously or over time.

> *Polygender*: Someone who experiences having multiple gender identities simultaneously or over time.

Muxe: A community/identity in Mexico that refers to a person who typically has male sexual characteristics, but identifies as female. The term originated with the Zapotec, a Native people of southern Mexico.

Neuroqueer: Someone whose identity, selfhood, gender

performance, and/or neurocognitive style have in some way been shaped by their engagement in practices of neuroqueering, regardless of what gender, sexual orientation, or style of neurocognitive functioning they may have been born with.

Neutrois: A nonbinary gender identity that falls under the genderqueer or transgender umbrellas. There is no one definition of Neutrois, since each person that self-identifies as such experiences their gender differently.

Nonbinary: Also referred to as "enby," this is a gender identity and umbrella term for gender identities that can't be exclusively categorized as man or woman.

Novigender: People who use this identity experience having a gender that can't be described using existing language due to its complex and unique nature.

Omnigender: Describes people who experience all or many identities on the gender spectrum simultaneously or over time.

Sekrata: A person who has male sexual characteristics, but after displaying behavior viewed as feminine during childhood, are raised as girls by their families. This identity belongs to the Sakalava people, who are indigenous to Madagascar.

Third Gender: Originating in non-Western and Indigenous cultures, this is a gender category that includes people who have a gender that can't be exclusively categorized as man or woman, or is different from man or woman.

Transmasculine: A person who was registered as female at birth but who lives and identifies as a man; aka a trans-man, transgender male, etc..

Transfemmine: A person who was registered as male at birth but who lives and identifies as a woman; aka a trans-woman, transgender female, etc.

Two Spirit: This umbrella term was created by Native American communities to bring traditional Indigenous understandings of gender and sexuality into Western and contemporary native education and literature. Two-spirit generally refers to a common, acknowledged, accepted, and praised gender classification among most First Nation communities, dating back centuries.

Violence Against Transgender Women

Many instances of violence against transgender women occur when cisgender heterosexual men are frustrated by their interest in a woman they don't initially recognize as transgender. In *Toxic Silence*, Dr. William T. Houston explains just how toxic masculinity has led to an increase in violence against trans-women, especially black trans-women, the group most likely to be murdered because of their gender identity:

"Toxic masculinity," which is a rebellious form of manhood that utilizes violence, is exercised by cisgender men who are attracted to transgender women but do not want their masculinity questioned. This is the root cause of the problem. These men are dating transgender women in secret and do not want anyone to know about these relationships. Then, when the men think it's possible it might become known, or if disclosure is threatened, they can become violent and kill the trans woman … I found that white cisgender men in relationships with black transgender women do not feel their masculinity is questioned as much as black cisgender men. For black cisgender men, challenging their masculinity could result in violence… Homosexuality is more accepted in the white community than in the black community… The social institution of the black church could be more involved in addressing the issues of black transgender women in a more positive way. In many respects, it is anti-LGBTQ and I view this as an epidemic. I believe the careless murder of human beings and the lack of ability to appreciate fellow human beings is an epidemic and it's the root of the problem.[1]

Many other arguments are used to dehumanize and invalidate transgender individuals. Some claim that transgender women are not "women" because they cannot carry a baby and give birth. While this is true, defining a woman by her ability to become pregnant excludes cisgender women who chose not to become mothers or who, for medical reasons, are unable to do so. Others suggest that gender transition is a joke. I have been told by people that if I can change my gender identity, they can identify as a cat! Transitioning genders is not changing into a different species—it is understanding, accepting, and acting on our internal sense of self.

Why, then, are arguments like these used to invalidate someone else's gender? Unfortunately, many people are only willing to accept what they understand. Those who have never experienced gender dysphoria, or who have never felt unable to express their natural sense of self, may find it difficult to understand why some people need to transition. Some cisgender men have difficulty accepting and affirming transgender individuals due to the narrow conception of their own sexuality. Keon West and Martha Lucia Borras-Guevara write in the *Journal of Homosexuality* that, "[w]hen the man discovers the woman is transgender, the man becomes threatened because of fear of being considered gay or queer, and therefore engages in discriminatory actions to try to counteract his previous sexual attraction to the woman. He does this because his limited concept of sexuality and gender causes him to believe he was being deceived by a man rather than seeing her as the woman she is."[2]

Many of those who seek to invalidate transgender lives do so mainly out of fear, or the limitations to their own sexuality, leading to hostility to all nonbinary identities. Cynthia Lee and Peter Kwan write that, "[m]en who have been aggressive toward transgender women have argued in their defense that having a sexual relationship with a transgender woman had felt like a 'theft of [their] heterosexuality.'"[3] We have seen instances of this repeatedly in television sitcoms, when male characters become agitated, or even attempt to engage in more "masculine" behaviors, after becoming aware that an attractive woman is actually transgender—and therefore a "man" in their eyes. A similar sense of confusion may occur when a cisgender heterosexual woman finds herself attracted to a transgender male. It is crucial that we move away from the traditional male/female binary concept of gender to one that is expansive and diverse.

What Does It Mean To Transition Genders?

Traditionally, a valid and successful transition meant undergoing the necessary medical and lifestyle changes to go from one gender binary to the other—male to female, or female to male. Why was this the common model of gender transition? It was for safety. In heteronormative cisnormative society, being recognized as either "male" or "female" made an individual less vulnerable to discrimination or abuse. Safety is still a legitimate concern; according to the Human Rights Campaign, in 2022, at least 40 transgender people were murdered due to their gender identity, while at least 32 died as a result of transphobic violence in 2023.[4] Each year on November 20, we recognize the transgender individuals we have lost to violence, suicide, and anti-trans hate during Transgender Day of Remembrance, which was started in 1999 by Gwendolyn Ann Smith:

> Transgender Day of Remembrance seeks to highlight the losses we face due to anti-transgender bigotry and violence. I am no stranger to the need to fight for our rights, and the right to simply exist is first and foremost. With so many seeking to erase transgender people—sometimes in the most brutal ways possible—it is vitally important that those we lose are remembered, and that we continue to fight for justice.[5]

Recently, increasing numbers of people have choosen to reject the traditional male/female binary entirely and transition as nonbinary. However someone decides to transition, it is important to emphasize that *the correct way to transition is the way that is best for that individual!*

How Does A Person Transition?

It is important to remember that gender transitioning is different for every person. Some transgender children and adults are happy to express their gender identity without any medical interventions, while others want to change their anatomy to match how they feel and wish to be seen. There is no set process. For example, when I came out in 2018, I first identified as a genderfluid cross-dresser. In this identity, I felt that I needed to dress in feminine clothing on occasion. As a result, on some days I aligned as a woman, wore women's attire, and used she/her pronouns, while on other days, I aligned more as a male and dressed as such, using he/him pronouns. For awhile, I felt like this was exactly what I needed to exist in my genderfluid identity. At the time, I was adamant that I did not wish to undergo any gender-affirming surgeries or hormone replacement therapy.

It wasn't until 2021 that I began to understand that my needs and understanding of my gender had changed. I had always been aware that part of my body was "missing," and that I felt most like myself when I wore breast forms. With the support of a therapist, I made the decision to undergo breast enhancement gender-affirming surgery. In February, 2022, the procedure took place at the Cleveland Clinic. After careful consideration, I decided to begin hormone replacement therapy in 2023. Overall, it took me about five years to feel that my body and mind were completely aligned. Today, I identify as transgender genderfluid and use they/she pronouns. I could not be happier.

Transgender people do not automatically understand exactly what they need to do in order to align themselves with their gender when they first come out. Like me, they all have a unique path and timeline to gender transition, evolving and changing in the hope that they we will eventually discover exacwhat they need in order to feel complete. There are also outside influences that can influence the process. For example, many people who are transitioning fear that they will be rejected by loved ones, and need time to seek out safe spaces and support from allies. Months of therapy may be necessary to help them feel comfortable with their decisions. The ever-changing political landscape may also affect a transgender person's sense of security, and play a role in their transition schedule.

Medical practitioners encourage their transgender patients to take the time to examine the long-term effects of gender-affirming surgeries or hormone replacement therapy. Those who argue against gender-affirming claim that people undergo medical procedures too quickly and then regret their choices and may decide to detransition later. According to GenderGP, 97 percent of transgender people are happy with gender-affirming medical procedures, with less than 3 percent regretting some part of their gender-affirming procedures.[6] There is no evidence that the 3 percent decide to detransition—only that they regret certain aspects of their medical care. For example, sometimes a transgender person begins hormone replacement therapy and discovers that they did not need it, or they have a medical procedure such as breast enhancement and realize that the implants do not help them align with their gender. Less than one percent of transgender people regret their decision enough to actually detransition.[7]

Social Transitioning

"Social transitioning" refers to the transitioning of a person's outward expression to the world. It can be as simple as changing clothing styles, or as impactful as changing one's pronouns and adopting a chosen name. Transgender people often go through multiple social transitions, changing aspects of their expression until they find what fits them best. Think of it like trying on a hat. Sometimes you find that perfect hat on the first try, while other times you have to try on several different hats until you find the right one.

It is important to understand that this is a process, and that everyone will go through their own social transition on their own timeline. The best way to be a supportive ally is to talk with the person and listen to how they are expressing themselves. It can be very damaging to tell the person that you liked the way they were before or during a different period of their social transition. Be supportive by showering them with unconditional love! This is often the time when a transgender person will also come out to the people in their lives. Remember that if you are fortunate enough to have a transgender person come out to you, be sure you don't betray their trust! You don't have the right to share this information with anyone unless that person has given you permission to do so.

Passing

Within the transgender community, you will often find that individuals are concerned with how well they "pass." This refers to a transgender individual being seen as a cisgender person at first glance. "Passing" is seen as a safety measure. Appearing to be cisgender lowers the risk of being treated differently or harassed. Rebecca Minor, a gender specialist, writes that, "[o]ne of the major reasons that passing can be so life-changing for trans people is that it can protect them from harm. A trans person who passes as cisgender is likely to face less prejudice, harassment, and risk of violence as a result of their gender presentation. In this way, trans people can feel pressure to pass, even if they would rather not have to."[8]

While passing may seem like a logical way to avoid discrimination and violence, it can actually be very damaging for a transgender person's mental health. When I first came out, I was obsessed with the idea of being seen as a cisgender woman. I wanted to blend in with the crowd and go unnoticed. My fear was that someone would recognize me as transgender and harass me for presenting myself as a gender different from my assigned sex at birth. I was so concerned with how well I passed that I ended up altering the expression of my gender identity to match traditional female beauty standards, rather than expressing myself truly. In public, I felt the need to look as "female" as possible. I am comfortable with my male anatomy, but I found myself "tucking" my male genitalia in order to pass. According to Trans Hub, "[t]he concept of passing places a burden of unrealistic gendered beauty standards on trans people, a standard that many cis people neither meet themselves or expect other cis people to meet."[9]

As we have seen, the need to adhere to traditional standards of beauty has damaged the self-esteem and mental health of many individuals. Placing even higher standards upon a transgender individual can be emotionally damaging. Pratyush Dayal of CBC News states that, "[n]arrow beauty standards can have serious impacts on body image for LGBTQ people, who already face higher rates of eating disorders and other mental illnesses. Further fuelling fears of not being accepted over their identity or orientation, some people can go to dangerous lengths to look a certain way."[10]

Being able to successfully pass as cisgender may be impacted by a number of factors, including a person's ability to access gender-affirming medical care, acquire gender-affirming clothing, make-up and hair products, the person's genetic background, and more. Rather than focusing on a transgender person's "success" in passing, we need to understand that gender expression varies from person to person, and that physical appearance is also deeply personal. Whether transgender or cisgender, you should have the freedom to express your gender identity as you see fit, not how others think you should.

The Pressures of Presentation

Just as with any person's public presentation and the expression of their individual personality, no single appearance is necessarily more authentic to one's gender identity. Is a woman wearing pants with a shirt and tie any less authentic than a woman wearing a dress? No. The way you present yourself doesn't define who you are. A transgender woman who has facial or body hair is no less authentic than a transgender woman who presents according to traditional gender norms. All trans-women are women, and all trans-men are men, no matter how they express and present their gender.

Some members of the transgender community believe that the only way to authentically transition is to do so "fully," which means using all methods, medically and socially, to live within a traditional gender binary. They suggest that transgender people are only "authentic" if they transition from male-to-female or female-to-male and adhere to the respective gender binaries. Individuals who have this viewpoint claim that all transgender people should follow the same steps as they seek to validate their gender identity. They believe that the time and work they put into transitioning from one binary gender to the other is belittled by those who chose a different journey. They also suggest that non-binary individuals harm the transgender community by making the concept of gender more difficult to understand, leading to additional discrimination against all transgender individuals.

However, this belief invalidates and dehumanizes nonbinary identities, as well as those transgender men and women who do not "completely" accept traditional gender binary norms. This idea also causes emotional damage to many transgender individuals. It is dangerous to perpetuate the idea that gender must be expressed as either "male" or "female" and that everyone must adhere to traditional gender presentations. Nonbinary people who have no desire to "choose" a specific gender identity deserve to live on their own terms, as their gender identities are just as valid as those of any other person.

Pressure to conform to traditional gender norms also perpetuates the belief that physical appearance is the most important aspect of a person. This leads to additional forms of discrimination based on one's attractiveness. Gender is an outward expression of one's identity, not a set of rules that govern a strictly binary existence. No matter how a person identifies their gender, they have the right to live in the manner that feels best to them. Men can wear dresses and makeup, women can wear suits and have facial/body hair. Your style is just one way to express yourself, so wear and express yourself in whatever makes you feel euphoric!

As an ally, you can help with this issue. National campaigns such as "Eff Your Beauty Standards" and "Love Your Body" have challenged harmful beauty standards, supporting positive self-image and body positivity for all. The goal of these campaigns is to create a world where passing is not needed—a world where everyone feels safe to appear exactly as they are. LGBTQIA+

rights activist Alok Vaid-Menon writes that, "[w]e should not have to approximate cis and white and binary standards of gender and beauty to be safe. We should not have to 'pass' in order to get home without being followed, or spat on, or worse. What if we are never going to look like women or men? That means that the harassment doesn't stop. There is no before or after there is just the terror."[11]

This would also require us to end "body shaming," which is the practice of criticizing people for falling short of the "perfect" images seen on television, film, and on social media. Body shaming is deeply harmful both to children and adults, and can be even more damaging when the criticism comes from loved ones, even when they think they are being helpful or offering advice. Instead, we should celebrate all bodies as good bodies. We should reject the pressure to conform to cisnormative body and beauty standards. It is important to celebrate transitioning bodies, rather than pushing people to "pass." Your transgender friends and family face a lot of body shaming and cisnormative beauty standards in their daily lives, so create a safe, judgment-free space that allows them to be exactly who they are.

The Intersex Community

Before we continue, it is important to talk about the intersex community and its connection to the transgender community. Intersex people are those whose genitalia, chromosomes, or reproductive organs differ from traditional male or female gender characteristics. Intersexuality is not uncommon—1 or 2 children out of every 100 are intersex, which is more common than the number of natural redheads.[12] Prior to the 1990s, intersexed people were typically referred to as "hermaphrodites."

There are many ways a person can be intersex. For example, some people are born with both male and female reproductive organs. In other instances, a child might have external female reproductive organs and therefore be assigned a female identity at birth, but also possess internal male organs, such as undescended testicles. According to The Cleveland Clinic,

> More recently, people who are intersex and advocates have spoken against intersex surgeries, calling them unnecessary. They want parents to let their children choose whether to get surgeries or treatments—and which ones—when they're old enough to make that choice. Many organizations, including the American Academy of Family Physicians, support intersex people in making decisions about their bodies. This means waiting until a person is old enough to give informed consent.[13]

At present, the proper procedure is for the doctor to explain to the parents that their newborn child is intersex. Parents are then advised to wait until puberty to determine whether any surgical alterations of the child's anatomy are needed.

Some intersex individuals find that the gender they were assigned at birth does not align with their identity as they reach puberty, and they may choose to transition. Other intersex people do not feel any need to transition, and are not transgender. No matter how an intersex person identifies their gender, it is important to understand the challenges they face, and to understand that their identity is valid. An intersex-inclusive pride flag was created in 2021 by artist Valentino Vecchietti (she/her) to confirm that intersex people are part of the LGBTQIA+ community and deserve to be valued and understood.[14]

Cross-Dressing

One segment of the LGBTQIA+ community that is often neglected or seen as invalid are those who cross-dress. A "cross-dresser" is a person who dresses in clothes associated with a different gender. Typically these are males who dress as a female, or vice versa. There are many different kinds of cross-dressing and several reasons why a person might engage in cross-dressing. At the heart of it, cross-dressing is simply an avenue of self-expression.

Cross-dressing has existed throughout history, like all LGBTQIA+ identities. Cross-dressers are not necessarily transgender, for they are not transitioning their gender from the one they were assigned at birth. Rather, cross-dressing is the practice of using clothing, makeup, wigs, etc., as an expression of personal style—not a sexual orientation.

Like many LGBTQIA+ individuals, a cross-dresser may feel the need to hide this part of themselves. You might equate cross-dressing to "drag," but the act of cross-dressing is not a "performance"—it is an expression of who the person is. Sometimes, a person who uses cross-dressing to express their personality might develop a new understanding of their gender and come out as transgender. This does not mean that all cross-dressers are transgender—rather that the practice is based on the lived experiences of each individual.

Society has traditionally mocked cross-dressers, which makes it difficult for them to be open about the practice. "Transvestite" has often been used to describe cross-dressers, though the term is outdated and widely considered to be derogatory.

Cross-dressing is part of the LGBTQIA+ spectrum and should be celebrated as such. As a result, allies should provide support for cross-dressers and respect their choices.

Gender Identity in Children

Many people believe that children are too young to understand their own gender identity, and thus expect them to adhere to the sex they are assigned at birth. Research, however, has shown otherwise, as children begin to realize their gender around age two, and have a stable grasp on their gender by age four.[15]

Children typically express their gender identity through

the toys they play with, the clothes they want to wear, their hairstyle, their chosen name, their social behaviors, and other outward expressions. According to Dr. Jason Rafferty of the Department of Pediatrics at the Warren Alpert Medical School of Brown University, "[w]hile a child's gender-specific behavior (i.e. gender expression) at any time seems to be influenced by exposure to stereotypes and their identification with the people in their lives, the internal sense of being a girl, boy, in between or something else (i.e. gender identity) cannot be changed."[16]

The school years play an important role in a child's gender exploration. Some schools place a high value on promoting a gender-affirming culture and building communities that allow students to understand and explore their LGBTQIA+ identity. These schools are seeking to help these students feel comfortable with who they are so that they can engage and learn more successfully in the classroom. For young children, gender transition is a social transition, which often involves a new haircut, a new name, and new clothes that match their gender identity. Adolescents may seek medical transition care such as hormone therapy or puberty blockers to assist them in aligning with their gender identity.[17]

Gender-affirming care by medical professionals is also critically important. According to the Office of Population Affairs of the US Department of Health and Human Services, "[f]or transgender and nonbinary children and adolescents, early gender-affirming care is crucial to overall health and well-being, as it allows the child or adolescent to focus on social transitions and can increase their confidence while navigating the healthcare system."[18] Appropriate medical care may help young people navigate difficult social challenges. The Trevor Project states that "[g]ender-affirming care can reduce the risk of suicide. One study found that transgender youth with access to gender-affirming hormones had a lower risk of suicide."[19]

While the following chapter discusses gender-affirming

health care in detail, I will discuss two of the most common forms of gender-affirming care provided to young people here, puberty blockers and hormone replacement therapy.

Puberty blockers, often the first medical step for transgender youth, stop older children from developing adult characteristics and are easily reversible. Once puberty blockers are stopped, a child's puberty begins. The Mayo Clinic states that puberty blockers are a safe way to help combat gender dysphoria in youth and do not cause any permanent damage.[20] Using puberty blockers is a great way to give young people and their families time to understand their gender, as well as the opportunity to determine what gender-affirming care might be needed. Other medical interventions are, for the most part, unavailable to minors.

Hormone Replacement Therapy (HRT), is somewhat reversible, but may cause some permanent effects, such as breast tissue growth in transgender girls. These treatments are generally used on older youth.

Remember that children have an understanding of their gender identity when they are very young. Listen to the way they describe themselves. Believe what they say. Ensure that their teachers and school administrators are committed to providing them with a safe and supportive environment. Offer them appropriate health care when needed. As an ally, be aware that giving a child the chance to explore their gender identity contributes to their health, happiness, and contentment.

Transgender Youth in Athletics

The debate regarding transgender athletes in sports has had a negative impact on LGBTQIA+ and cisgender athletes alike. The belief that transgender females have a competitive advantage over cisgender athletes has led to the removal of some young players from school teams. The ACLU has noted, however, that a person's genetic makeup does not determine their athletic success. Trans athletes vary in athletic ability, just like their cisgender counterparts.[21] Dr. Deanna Adkins of the Duke Child and Adolescent Gender Care Clinic adds that, "[w]hen a school or athletic organization denies transgender students the ability to participate equally in athletics because they are transgender, that condones, reinforces, and affirms the transgender students' social status as outsiders or misfits who deserve the hostility they experience from peers."[22] In other words, it encourages cisgender students to mistreat their classmates.

It is important to push back against the idea that any young athlete would transition in order to "win." Gender dysphoria is psychologically debilitating, and no athlete would willingly "choose" to transition genders just to play a sport. The hostility they experience is challenging enough without the added pressures of "faking" an identity. Remember that gender transition is not a "trend," a "fad," or "attention-seeking behavior." It is a means of survival.

Transgender Identities in Adult Athletics

The claim that transgender women have a physical advantage over cisgender women in women's sports also leads to discrimination against all athletes. Let's look at an example from the 2024 Summer Olympic games in Paris. A post on the social media platform X by the author J.K Rowling, well known for her transphobic statements, sparked an outcry by claiming that two boxers, Algeria's Imane Khelif and Twiwan's Lin Yu Ting, were men competing against women. Both athletes were subjected to tests that detected the presence of XY chromosomes in their genetic makeup, leading to the belief by some that they should be banned from participating in the boxing events. Khelif and Yu Ting were in fact assigned female identities at birth, underwent hormone testing for their testosterone levels, and were cleared for competition by the International Olympic Committee.[23]

Being born with XX chromosomes does not necessarily make someone a woman, just as being born with XY chromosomes does not make a person a man. Human beings can be born with chromosomal variations, including having multiple X and Y chromosomes.[24] A person's sex assigned at birth does not inherently advantage or disadvantage them in competition; it is simply one of many elements that make up who they are. There are several factors that contribute to an athlete's ability to succeed in competition: biology, time, resources, training and money, to name a few. Examples of athletes who have biological advantages in competition include

- Michael Phelps, who excels at swimming in part because his wingspan is longer than his height. He is also hyper-jointed in the chest, meaning he can kick from his chest instead of just his ribs. His double-jointed ankles bend 15 percent more than his rivals and, coupled with his size fourteen feet, help his legs act like flippers to glide him through the water.

- At 4-foot-8, Simone Biles' height-to-strength ratio enables her to do more flips/maneuvers in the same amount of time as other gymnasts who might be taller.

- The late Manute Bol, at 7 feet 7 inches, was the tallest person to ever play in the NBA (tied with Gheorghe Mureşan). Bol was widely considered one of the best shot-blockers in NBA history—a title he earned, in part, because of his height. [25]

Despite these facts, the idea persists that some female athletes are actually "men" and should be banned from sports in order to protect other women. In order to compete as a transwoman in women's sports, one must undergo hormone replacement therapy and have a verified testosterone level equal to that of a cisgender woman. Simply put, transphobic narratives continue to plague female athletes.

Let's Look in the Mirror

Before I wrap up this section, I want to invite you to explore and gain a better understanding of your gender. I am not going to try to convince you that you are transgender, or that you should transition genders—rather, I want you to examine how you define your gender. Those of us who are transgender have spent a lot of time exploring our gender and developing our definition of our gender. I want you to do the same because we all have a gender identity.

Here is the question:

How would you define your gender in terms other than by your genitalia?

For example, you cannot state, "I am a man because I have a penis." The body parts and sexual organs you possess do not determine your gender. Instead, it is an innate feeling and understanding of how you see yourself, and how you express yourself to the world.

Below are examples from some friends of mine:

Shannon Taylor (He/Him/His): "I am a man because when I see myself in the mirror, through my own eyes, I see a man and feel it in my heart."

Deborah Pohlot (She/Her/They/Them): "I define my gender as a nonbinary person by my grace, courage, mindfulness, and style."

Zac Boyer (They/Them/Theirs): "I'm nonbinary in that I

straddle the line of femininity and masculinity in both my spirit and my body. I can say this confidently now, but this hasn't always been the case. People tried to stifle the feminine in me and in many ways haven't stopped trying to chip away those bits they deem inappropriate. I'm grateful I can continue tuning out those perspectives and focus on my inner voice, the quiet confidence of knowing I'm exactly the way I'm meant to be—an ever flowing stream of all genders, crashing into each other like waves of sea foam; beauty, strength, and chaos all in harmony."

Noyka Latte (She/Her): "I think being a woman is not at all about what it used to be. Women have multiple hats we have to wear every day. Not to mention being picked on for being 'too emotional' or 'too sensitive.' A lot of times in my life when I was told as a woman that I needed to develop thicker skin—especially in a male dominant workforce—it would always offend me! Why do I need to 'toughen up' instead of the men 'lightening up'? Or when I was a kid I didn't play football, I did cheerleading, because 'think about where those little boys are putting their hands.'

We are always urged to steer from the direction of 'hard work' or 'tough job,' when some of the strongest people I know are women. Being a woman is more than just having a vagina and a uterus. I strongly believe that feminine energy is truly what all these people mean when they say, 'you fight like a girl,' or 'you cry like a woman,' because at the end of the day, it's not the woman that's soft, it's the feminine energy. And what's most beautiful about that is everyone has divine feminine energy inside them no matter the gender. It's what makes your heart warm when you see your mom smile. It's what motivates you to make a house into a home. It's that guilty pleasure to sing show tunes you sing in the car by yourself.

Being a divine feminine is not about having a vagina or uterus or even giving birth to a baby! Being a woman is about finding the yin in every yang. It's about opening up new perspectives, not muting them. To learn about yourself so you are able to love endlessly. Gender is no longer a deciding factor in what is and is not a man or a woman. I fix cars, I unclog drains, I ride motorcycles, and I cuss like a sailor, but I'm a woman in all my beautiful divine MASCULINE AND FEMININE energy.

I would never back down from a challenge or opportunity to make the world better. I think that's what being a woman is all about. Being strong when everyone expects you to fail. Pushing and persevering, even when the weight of the world seems too heavy. You don't need fallopian tubes to ride the waves and you don't need a uterus to be a homemaker. You just need to know your soul is stronger than any title anyone tries to put on you.

Sam Shim (He/Him/His): "I am a man because my brain tells me that my identity is a male. It has nothing to do with my DNA or my physical attributes. These traits do not define my gender. In childhood, I was raised as a boy, and I always felt comfortable being a male. But I also would have what some in society would consider 'feminine' traits such as empathy and dress. Twenty years ago, I embraced the term metrosexual to summarize me. I am secure in who I am, and I feel that toxic masculinity is a major issue in our society."

Take some time and reflect upon these examples. Truly think

about what it is that makes you the gender that you understand yourself to be. In doing so, I promise you that you will have a greater appreciation for those who have to spend years living as the wrong gender, only to finally be able to transition and live as they have known themselves to be. Each individual has their own definitions and lived experiences, which help to shape their understanding of their gender. In order to be an ally to the LGBTQIA+ community, you have to be respectful, understanding, and willing to learn.

Summary: Understanding and Supporting Gender Transitioning

This chapter offers fact-based information on the following subjects:

- The Transgender Umbrella
- Terms Currently Used to Describe Transgender Identities
- Facts About Gender Transition
- The Experience of Transition
- How Does a Person Transition?
- Social Transitioning
- Passing
- The Pressures of Presentation
- Pushing Back Against Standards of Beauty
- The Intersex Community
- Gender Identity in Children
- Transgender Youth in Athletics
- Transgender Identities in Adult Athletics
- Examine Your Own Gender

5. Gender-Affirming Medical Care

"No. I have never regretted receiving gender-affirming care. It is honestly the best thing that happened in my life." —Amy Schneider, *Jeopardy!* champion

Imagine this scenario: A cisgender woman wants to have breast enhancement or reduction surgery to help her feel more comfortable in her body. She is able to schedule an appointment with a doctor, explain her reasoning, and then get a referral to a surgeon for the procedure, usually without any issue. A transgender individual, on the other hand, must fulfill a long list of requirements before they are eligible to get the same surgery. And, despite these hurdles, many still end up not receiving care. Both the cisgender woman and the transgender person want to have the same surgery performed for similar reasons, yet the steps to receiving medical care for each are vastly different.

Why is that? Mainly due to misinformation surrounding gender-affirming care—in particular, that transgender people are not mentally "fit" to make medical decisions concerning their own care. This could not be further from the truth. Transgender identities are not a mental health disease, and those who seek gender-affirming care are not mentally ill. While this claim has been repeatedly debunked, too many still believe it. This in turn affects the care that transgender individuals receive.

Most transgender people have to wait months, if not years, to receive gender-affirming medical care. For example, in 2024 the private health insurance company Aetna had the following requirements before an individual was permitted to receive gender-affirming medical procedures:

- Signed letter or referral from a qualified mental health professional.

- Persistent, well-documented gender dysphoria.

- The capacity to make a fully-informed decision and to consent to treatment.

- Six months of continuous hormone therapy as appropriate to the member's gender goals.

- Consent of a parent or legal guardian for those less than eighteen years of age, as well as completion of hormone replacement therapy for an average of twelve months.

- If significant medical or mental health concerns are present, the symptoms must be reasonably well controlled.[1]

Let's take a deeper look into each of these requirements, which while based on Aetna's standards, are similar for other insurance companies, as well as government-based healthcare in other countries.

Referral From A Mental Health Professional

An individual must provide documentation from a licensed therapist that understands the pros and cons of gender-affirming surgery, have the mental capacity to make informed decisions about their body, and benefit from gender-affirming treatment. In some states, such as Ohio, the individual also needs a letter of support from their primary care physician.

Documentation of Gender Dysphoria

Gender dysphoria is a sense of ongoing, acute anxiety experienced by individuals whose gender and sexual identities do not align with the sex assigned to them at birth. An individual must provide records from doctors, therapists, or other mental health professionals attesting to their long-term struggles with the condition. This may be difficult because many people are hesitant to share their sense of gender dysphoria with others, fearing criticism and rejection.

The Capacity to Make A Fully-Informed Decision and to Consent to Treatment

Before performing gender-affirming surgeries, doctors must feel that an individual understands the mental and physical effects of the procedure. A medical intervention may require post-surgical treatment, rehabilitation, and psychological counseling. Individuals should consider how the surgery will affect their relationships with friends, family members, and colleagues. The individual should also consider the cost of treatment and how it will be managed if the surgery requires them to miss work. In short, careful consideration should be given to both the immediate and long-term changes, both positive and negative, that gender-affirming medical care might bring to a person's life.

Six Months of HRT (Twelve Months for Minors)

Some insurance companies and medical providers require a transgender individual to receive Hormone Replace Therapy (HRT) for a period of time, while others do not. This is due to the fact that HRT changes an individual's weight and body shape, which may have an effect on the surgery.[2] This is not the case with all patients, and was not the case with my surgery. Sometimes, patients are able to forgo this "requirement," depending on their gender identity and medical needs.

Consent For Minors

Individuals under the age of eighteen are not eligible for gender-affirming surgeries in many states, although some do allow minors to receive surgery with parental/guardian consent.

Keep in mind that if a doctor or surgeon feels like the patient does not adhere to any or all of these steps, the procedure can be canceled.

My Personal History

In 2021, I met with my primary care physician and mental health care team and we determined that I needed breast enhancement surgery in order to align my body to my gender. I then met with a surgeon who determined that the procedure was appropriate for me.

After obtaining the required documents and receiving approval from my health insurance, I met with my surgeon a week before the scheduled date to go over the details of the procedure and the recovery period. During this meeting, my surgeon informed me that my surgery would be canceled because she felt "I did not understand the ramifications of having this surgery." I had fulfilled all the pre-op requirements set by the State of Ohio and my health insurance, yet my surgeon decided to cancel the procedure. Unfortunately, this situation happens to a lot of transgender individuals, with 55 percent being denied care.[3]

I finally underwent breast enhancement surgery in 2022.

Minors and Gender-Affirming Surgery

Many states have enacted bans on gender-affirming care for minors, stating that they are too young to understand the long term effects of such medical procedures. As of January 2024, the following states have bans: Alabama, Arkansas, Arizona, Florida, Georgia, Iowa, Idaho, Indiana, Kentucky, Louisiana, Missouri, Mississippi, Montana, North Carolina, North Dakota, Nebraska, Ohio, Oklahoma, South Dakota, Tennessee, Texas, Utah, and West Virginia.[4] Some of these states, including my home state of Ohio, have a grandfather clause permitting the continuation of gender affirming care for minors who began treatment before the law was enacted.

The bans also affect minors whose parents and legal guardians are in favor of gender-affirming care. This means that young people, including those who have adult support, do not have the right to make informed decisions about their own lives. Some researchers believe that this is a mistake. Petronella Grootens-Wiegers, a research associate in health communication and ethics, writes that, "[e]mpirical evidence demonstrates that children have an emerging competence at a very young age. Weithorn & Campbell found children as young as 9 years old to have the capacity to make informed choices In addition, some studies conclude that children at age 14 or 15 are as competent as adults."[5]

Recent laws also prohibit minors from receiving hormone treatments and puberty blockers, as well as gender-affirming surgeries. Puberty blockers are a safe and effective way to delay the onset of puberty to allow a transgender child to maintain their gender identity. There is no evidence that they are harmful, and they can be discontinued if necessary.

The use of hormones in gender-affirming care also assists minors in aligning their bodies with their gender identities. Forbidding these medications to minors prevents them from successfully transitioning, which can increase their gender dysphoria, with damaging consequences.

In most situations, hormones and gender-affirming surgeries are not prescribed to anyone under the age of eighteen. It is only in rare cases, and under the supervision of a team of medical providers, that such care is provided. According to the Office of Population Affairs (OPA),

Research demonstrates that gender-affirming care improves the mental health and overall well-being of gender-diverse children and adolescents. Because gender-affirming care encompasses many facets of healthcare needs and support, it has been shown to increase positive outcomes for transgender and nonbinary children and adolescents. Gender-affirming care is patient-centered and treats individuals holistically, aligning their outward, physical traits with their gender identity.[6]

The following table comes from OPA's 2022 guide on gender-affirming care and young people. The table indicates the optimal age when certain gender-affirming care procedures should take place, and whether or not they are reservable. No matter what your personal views or beliefs are on this matter, it is important to remember that medical decisions are private, and should remain the domain of individuals and their physicians. We should trust that the medical providers and parents of trangender youth understand what is best for their children.

Affirming Care	What is it?	When is it used?	Reversible or not
Social Affirmation	Adopting gender-affirming hairstyles, clothing, name, gender pronouns, and restrooms and other facilities	At any age or stage	Reversible
Puberty Blockers	Using certain types of hormones to pause pubertal development	During puberty	Reversible
Hormone Therapy	Testosterone hormones for those who were assigned female at birth Estrogen hormones for those who were assigned male at birth	Early adolescence onward	Partially reversible
Gender-Affirming Surgeries	"Top" surgery – to create male-typical chest shape or enhance breasts "Bottom" surgery – surgery on genitals or reproductive organs Facial feminization or other procedures	Typically used in adulthood or case-by-case in adolescence	Not reversible

US Department of Health and Human Services, Office of Population Affairs[7]

Raven's Story

To help us understand the need for transgender minors to receive gender-affirming care, I share the story of Raven, a transgender youth in Ohio. His story is one of perseverance and self-discovery in the face of horrible discrimination and hate.

Raven (He/Him)

My gender transition journey began when I was twelve years old, when I came out to my parents on a flight home from Arizona. I did not come out as transgender, but rather told my parents that I wasn't straight. I did not know exactly what that meant at the time; however, I knew that the straight thing was not who I was. It took me years of growing to understand who I was, and to understand how my gender and sexuality aligned with my identity. Today, at seventeen, I am trans-masculine.

During my years of transitioning, I went through a process of figuring myself out, sort of like trying on different clothing styles. I began identifying as queer, then non-binary, and now trans-masculine. My journey does not invalidate who I was at the time, as I used terms and identities that best represent[ed] who I was at that time. Growing and understanding oneself takes many years, and I am proud of my journey to get to who I am today.

It was not all great, however. My parents were there to support me and love me unconditionally the whole time, but there were others who sought to tear me down. When I started high school, that was when I began to reinvent myself, using the lived name "Raven" and presenting myself as more masculine. Being a high schooler and transitioning genders is no easy task, and some of my peers went out of their way to discriminate against me. In Ohio, our politicians have sought to ban gender-affirming care for minors, and have created a toxic and dangerous culture for us to survive in. One of their bills sought to ban transgender youth from playing sports on the team that aligned with their gender; meaning that since I am assigned female at birth (AFAB), I must play on the girls teams.

Complying with this, I played on the girls' volleyball

team. It was already hard enough for me to play on the girls' team, as I felt like I did not belong and could not connect with the girls on the team. This, though, was seen as a violation to my peers, as a group of boys created a petition to have me removed from the team because I am trans. They protested my participation and created a dangerous environment where I constantly feared for my safety—so much so that I eventually left the team. I had not been receiving any gender-affirming care—I was just identifying my gender as masculine. I was following the rules that the Ohio politicians created, yet I was still being discriminated against.

Bathrooms have always been a precarious place for me as well. Being that I identify as transmasc, I feel that I am invading women's spaces when entering a girl's restroom. I am constantly tense and on guard, always fearing that someone will take offense and become violent towards me, just because I am using the bathroom.

I transitioned because this is who I am, not because I was following a fad or rushing into a decision. I took years to understand myself and grow in my gender identity. Watching transgender creators and influencers on social media platforms definitely helped me realize that I was transgender, but they did not influence me into making a decision that was not my own. Rather they helped me understand that it was perfectly normal to not feel like a girl, and that there was nothing wrong with me for feeling more masculine.

So the entire time throughout my transition, nothing has been set in stone. It's always just been I'm not this, so let's find what I am. It's a journey and there was a time in my transition that I've been nonbinary. Then I've been nonbinary leaning masculine and then I've been transmasc. While my understanding of my gender has changed, there hasn't been a time that I've ever regretted my transition.

Yes, I was not in the binary, and that's what made me feel comfortable. I have no regrets about that and I feel like if someone has the opportunity to be comfortable in who they are, then they should have the opportunity to become who they are. Many will claim that I am too young to make a decision like this; to them I say this: I understand myself far better than you will, and I will decide what is best for me.

The Takeaway

With all of this information, what can you do as an ally?

First, gaining an understanding of gender transitioning is key. Research what transgender people go through on a daily basis—from the rise of anti-transgender legislation, to ongoing daily hostility, to the steps required to obtain appropriate health care. Understand that transgender people do not transition their gender to seek fame, win at sports, or for "fun." They transition because it is what they need to do in order to feel at home in their bodies.

Second, understand what it means to experience gender dysphoria. Think of it like wearing a pair of shoes. If you're wearing shoes that fit perfectly, you don't even think about them. That is what life is like when you don't experience gender dysphoria. Now imagine those shoes fit badly. Maybe they're a bit too small or too big. Maybe one has a rock stuck in the sole. As you walk around, you constantly think about them. You might be able to ignore your discomfort for a time, but you are always aware that the shoes don't fit. Eventually you can't stop thinking about taking off the shoes. Making yourself comfortable. Perhaps you can keep the same shoes by having them repaired. Or maybe you need an entirely new pair.

That is what gender dysphoria feels like for a transgender individual. Your body does not align to your gender. Every person experiences gender dysphoria in their own unique way. One person might struggle with their appearance and choose to undergo facial feminization/masculinization surgery. Another person might only need to change their wardrobe in order to align their expression with their gender identity. The best way you can support someone experiencing gender dysphoria is to listen to them, believe them, and support them in what they need.

Don't Forget To...

- Support someone in their gender transition by showing them unconditional love.
- Allow others to live their lives in a manner that feels right for them.
- Believe them as they journey through their transition.
- Understand that they face criticism and discrimination.
- Treat them with empathy and respect.
- Avoid preconceived ideas about the process or transition, or transgender identities.
- Listen. Transgender individuals face many challenges.
- Educate yourself about transgender experiences.
- Challenge unfair acts, unkind remarks, and discriminatory behavior toward transgender individuals.

Remember that a transgender person is still the person you knew before. You are not losing that person. *If anything, your relationship will only grow and become stronger.*

Summary: Gender-Affirming Medical Care

The Process of Receiving Gender-Affirming Medical Care

- A referral from a mental health professional.

- Documentation of gender dysphoria

- The capacity to make a fully-informed decision and to consent to treatment.

- Minors must have the consent of a parent or legal guardian.

- Six months of continuous hormone therapy as appropriate to the member's gender goals, twelve months for minors.

- If a doctor or surgeon feels like the patient at any time does not adhere to any of these steps, the procedure can be canceled.

6. Understanding Sexuality

"There will not be a magic day when we wake up and it's now okay to express ourselves publicly. We make that day by doing things publicly until it's simply the way things are."—Tammy Baldwin, first openly gay United States Senator

Sexuality is an important part of a person's identity. Discovering and understanding your sexuality can be an extremely liberating and exciting process, yet can also cause one to become the target of discrimination.

Let's first discuss our current understanding of "sexuality." Often the term is used to describe someone's sexual attraction to others, and how often a person engages in sexual activity. I will discuss the complexities of sexual attraction before turning to issues surrounding sexual activity.

The Sexuality "Spectrum"

The sexuality "spectrum" is just as diverse as the transgender "umbrella," and can be just as confusing for those who are not familiar with it. In the past, it was generally believed that all humans experienced sexual attraction within the male/female binary. Today we understand that sexual identities—and sexual attraction—fall within a "spectrum" and resists easy classification. Instead of offering people a choice between either homosexual or heterosexual—or even a choice between homosexual, heterosexual, and bisexual—the "spectrum" recognizes a wide range of sexual identities and behaviors. Sexual attraction is not necessarily synonymous with sexual activity. One can experience attraction mentally and emotionally, as well as physically. In some cases, such as with asexual identities, sexual attraction involves no physical activity at all. The sexuality spectrum allows for greater fluidity of sexual identity and expression.

The list below defines some of the various sexual identities:

Asexual: A spectrum of identities relating to individuals who experience little or no sexual attraction to others of any gender.

Aromatic: A spectrum of identities relating to individuals who experience little or no romantic attraction, regardless of sex or gender.

Bisexual: A sexual orientation that describes people who experience sexual, romantic, or emotional attraction to people of more than one gender.

Biromantic: Someone who experiences romantic attraction, but not sexual attraction, to people of more than one gender.

Demisexual: This sexual orientation describes people who experience sexual attraction only under specific circumstances, such as after building a romantic or emotional relationship with a person.

Gay / Lesbian / Homosexual: Describes people who experience sexual, romantic, or emotional attraction to people of the same or a similar gender.

Graysexual: Acknowledges the gray area on the sexuality spectrum for people who don't explicitly and exclusively identify as asexual or aromantic.

Heterosexual: Describes people who experience sexual, romantic, or emotional attraction to people of the "opposite" gender (e.g., male with female, man with woman) or a different gender. Both cisgender and transgender-identified people can be heterosexual. This sexual orientation category is commonly described as straight.

Omnisexual: Used to describe people whose sexuality isn't limited to those of a particular gender, sex, or sexual orientation.

Pansexual: People who can experience sexual, romantic, or emotional attraction to any person, regardless of that person's gender, sex, or sexuality.

Polysexual: Describes people with a sexual orientation that involves sexual or romantic attraction to people with varying gender.

Misunderstanding Sexual Activity in the LGBTQIA+ Community

The term "sexuality" has recently become synonymous with "sexual activity." This unfortunately means that some people attach non-traditional sexuality with certain prejudices and misinformation used against the LGBTQIA+ community.

One common misconception of LGBTQIA+ life is that members of the community are sexually deviant and highly promiscuous. This idea forms the basis of much of the anti-LGBTQIA+ legislation being enacted across the United States. The unfounded claim that the LGBTQIA+ community wants to indoctrinate children to their way of life has led to the recent banning of drag events, such as story times for young children. The ongoing debate about transgender individuals' use of public bathrooms is driven by the idea that a transgender person might enter a bathroom with the deliberate intention of sexually assaulting a woman or child. These fears represent the false belief that members of the LGBTQIA+ community are unable to control their sexual desires, and therefore engage in reprehensible acts, posing a threat to society.

Let's look at the origin of these fears about the LGBTQIA+ community.

Heteronormativity

Our society is built on the idea that heterosexuality is "normal," and that people should identify as either male or female (the gender "binary"), and be "cis-gender," or aligned to the sex assigned to them at birth. Our societal bias toward heteronormativity leads to many misconceptions about the realities of gender and sexuality.

The first misconception is that there are only two genders, male and female, and that all people are cisgender. However, it is incorrect to assume that all people are heterosexual ("straight") and are only attracted to those of the "opposite" sex. It is equally untrue that people must adhere to the roles constructed by society and associated with their assigned gender. Heteronormativity forms the basis of much of the hatred and discrimination directed towards LGBTQIA+ individuals. The pressure to conform to heteronormative beliefs causes many LGBTQIA+ people to undergo painful struggles with self-understanding, self-expression, and self-respect.

How do we break this cycle? It first comes from accepting that not everyone experiences attraction in the same way. Some experience attraction towards a different gender, some the same gender, others experience attraction towards multiple genders, and some do not experience attraction at all. No matter how someone experiences and expresses their attraction is valid. Anytime we as a society mandate that everyone express themselves in the same way, we destroy what is truly beautiful about being human. As people, we have an amazing ability of metacognition, which allows us to process our inner thoughts and feelings. This means that each person has the possibility of expressing their inner self and sharing it, in the manner they choose, with the world. This should be celebrated, as it is what makes us unique, and different from all other species.

Why is attraction so important in our society? From my personal experience, the answer is quite simple…sex. Our sexual identity plays an important role in our life, determining how we see and are seen by others. We treat those who we find attractive with more interest and respect than others. However, our heteronormative culture often creates barriers to anything but "straight" expression. Consider the following situation:

Two cisgender men are in a bar. Bob is a heterosexual male and Jim is a homosexual male. Neither is aware of how the other identifies. In talking, Jim mentions that he thinks Bob is attractive. Bob immediately becomes hostile and walks away.

Jim has done absolutely nothing wrong in expressing his attraction to Bob. In fact, it is quite common for heterosexual men like Bob to approach women, even strangers, and openly express their attraction to them. Bob's negative reaction to Jim's comment was likely driven by his fear that he might be seen as gay—a challenge to his sexual identity—and a sign of his heteronormative bias against other sexualities.

Now let's imagine that the same situation unfolds differently:

Two cisgender men are in a bar. Bob is a heterosexual male and Jim is a homosexual male. Neither is aware of how the other identifies. In talking, Jim mentions that he thinks Bob is attractive. Bob explains that he is attracted to women, but thanks Jim for the compliment. The two men carry on their conversation and enjoy the evening.

This situation ends positively because Bob feels comfortable in his sexual identity and experiences no bias against other sexualities. Bob responds to Jim with respect, avoiding any hostility.

The Sexual Spectrum is Fluid

Sexuality does not exist as a binary—male or female, heterosexual or homosexual—but is a spectrum spread across many different forms and expressions. There are many valid ways to identify and express one's attraction towards others. Not all feelings of attraction involve physical desire. While gender can play into sexuality, gender does not define one's sexuality. Rather, gender and sexuality are two aspects of human life. There can be many different ways of experiencing one's sexual identity, and all are meaningful and valid.

It's also important to understand that sexuality is fluid, and can change and evolve over time. This means that a person's sexual identity may shift during their lifetime. Attraction to others can change based on an individual's experiences and expressions. A person can come out as homosexual and identify that way for years, then have their attractions change to a point where they might begin to identify as bisexual. This doesn't mean that everyone's sexual attractions will change, just that those whose attractions do change are valid in their sexual identity.

Remember that a person's sexuality is whatever they say it is. Oftentimes, when a person is bisexual, pansexual, asexual, etc., some consider their identity invalid. For example, a bisexual woman who is in a relationship with a cisgender man is not "heterosexual"—she is still bisexual, and is engaged in a relationship that some may view as hetronormative. The relationship does not define a person's sexual identity.

As well, a person who is asexual or aromantic—that is, not engaged in sexual activity—may be in a relationship with someone. That does not invalidate their sexual identity, it just means that they found a person or persons whom they can share their life with. Be aware that individuals do not have to justify

104

their sexuality to you. They do not need to validate their identity by being in a relationship that neatly aligns with their sexual identity. Sexuality is a part of who they are, but it is not all of who they are.

Being respectful of someone's sexual identity is a great start, but it is only part of the picture. To be a true ally you must be willing to learn and understand. Education comes in many different forms, but is much more than just a Google search to learn the dictionary definition of someone's identity. Be open to challenges faced by the entire LGBTQIA+ community when it comes to the meaning of sexuality.

Now, let's direct our attention to understanding and empathizing with the lived experiences of LGBTQIA+ individuals when expressing their sexuality. I'll start!

My Personal History

I am a transgender lesbian, meaning that while I have transitioned from being assigned male at birth, I am attracted to women. My lesbian identity is not defined by an attraction to cisgender women, though I am happily married to one. I find all forms and expressions of femininity to be attractive. I do not act upon this because I am in a monogamous relationship, but my sexual attraction is completely valid. I have always been attracted to femininity, beginning in puberty and continuing through my gender transition. Therefore, I do not have a wide variety of lived experiences to share about my sexuality.

Some people believed that after I transitioned genders my sexuality would have transitioned to an attraction to masculinity. It is common for people to assume that transgender individuals experience a transition in their sexuality to align with their chosen gender. This is due to the hetronormative binary that permeates our culture. My gender has had no effect on my sexuality, and vice versa. I have always been attracted to femininity because that is where my feelings and thoughts of attraction lead me. To assume that one's gender must determine their sexuality leads to continuing misunderstandings about the LGBTQIA+ community. Remember that someone's gender and sexuality are unique to them, and can be different, even in similarly identifying individuals.

I would like to take some time here to share the narratives of some friends of mine, Reverend Brandon Robertson (He/Him), Cody Daigle-Orians (They/Them), and Rebecca Minor (She/Her/They). I share their stories with their permission, as examples of the different lived experiences of those within the LGBTQIA+ community.

Reverend Brandon Robertson (He/Him)

Coming out as a queer Christian man was not an easy journey. I had been told, in no uncertain terms, exactly what it means to be a "Christian man" by my pastors and Bible college professors, yet I could never actually live up to their standards of "biblical masculinity" because it was not who I was. I knew that I didn't choose to be "different"—this was just how God made me—and despite many attempts to conform to this definition of manhood and sexuality, nothing seemed to work. When I finally did come out as openly gay, I faced enormous backlash—I was told I was indulging the flesh, not willing to "crucify" my desires for the sake of faithfulness to Christ. This caused me much second-guessing and shame, but ultimately I knew that I was simply being who I was, and because we believe all humans are made in God's image, it seemed to me that who I was must also be a reflection of who God is.

The more I studied Scripture and the Christian tradition, the more I realized that modern Christian teaching about sexuality and gender had no basis in good scholarship or even the best modern psychology—they were beliefs rooted in patriarchy, bias, and fragile masculinity. Yet even today, as I stand proudly as a queer Christian pastor, I continue to receive the ire of conservative men, primarily. I believe this is because queerness is a threat to them—their faith is rooted in patriarchy, and queerness threatens the arbitrary assumptions that patriarchy requires to function. When queer people claim their place in the church, they expose the lies that the church has perpetuated about sexuality and gender as a means to control people. Queer people, our lives, and our love are examples of the radical, untamable nature of our Creator, who cannot be contained by doctrines or dogmas or human-crafted ideas of who people should be and how we should express ourselves in the world.

The more free I am to express my unique queer identity, and the more liberated I am to reclaim the Bible as a queer text, the more anger and fear I experience from the non-affirming church. But this seems like exactly what Jesus did in his day—challenged age old religious assumptions with provocations that called people to move outside of their boundaries and borders and into the "kingdom of God"—the world, and humanity, as we were created to be, living and loving freely, in our diversity, as a reflection of God's own creativity.

Cody Diagle-Orians (They/Them)

Living authentically as an ace (asexual) individual was not something I discovered until later in life. For most of my life, I considered myself to be a bad gay man, someone who found attraction in connection with other men, but not sexual attraction. I was convinced that there had to be something wrong with me, as I did not long for the sexual intimacy that society had convinced me we all longed for.

It was not until I was forty years old did I discover that my non-desire for sexual attraction was normal, and meant that I am asexual. I am married to a wonderful man, and also engaged in another polyamorous relationship with a man. While I do not experience sexual attraction to either of them, it has not

THE QUEER ALLIES BIBLE

limited our ability to grow a healthy and beautiful relationship. My desires are to build a relationship and partnership with the men I love.

Many people believe that asexual individuals prefer to be alone and not engage in any type of intimate relationship. While that may be true for some, it is not true for all. As well, asexual individuals are not necessarily driven to other asexuals. As is in my case, I am married to and in a relationship with another gay man. Both men are physically attracted to other men. While sexual intimacy is sometimes part of my relationships, it is more about expressing my love for them rather than achieving any sexual gratification. My asexuality is a part of me, not a bug or a problem that needs to be addressed and fixed. I am very lucky to have partners who see it that way and embrace me for who I am.

For asexual individuals, respect is key. Having a meaningful and deep relationship with an asexual individual or as an asexual individual is more than possible just as long as respect is given. Remember that as humans we are all different, and experience attraction, love, and desire uniquely. No matter how you identify, remember that your sexuality is valid and needs to be respected by all.

Rebecca Minor (She/Her/They)

It took me a long time to recognize and claim my identity as queer. As a teenager, I felt attraction to people of various genders, but due to compulsory heterosexuality and the stigma of bisexuality, I only dated guys. My freshman year of college, a course called "Queer and Pleasant Danger" opened my eyes to queer theory and the expansive nature of identity. Even then, I didn't feel like I could claim a queer identity because of my cisgender male partner, despite spending most of my time in queer spaces with queer folks. I was out to my boyfriend (now spouse) and friends, but not to family or the public because it didn't feel like it mattered.

Eventually, after working as a therapist for years and encouraging young people to live their truth, I knew I had to live mine. Now, I live openly and authentically as a queer femme regardless of my spouse, despite us being perceived as a heterosexual couple. While I recognize the privilege of being in a straight-presenting relationship, there is also an erasure of identity. The challenges I faced in coming out were not from friends or family, but from gatekeeping within the LGBTQ+ community because I'm married to a cisgender man. This gatekeeping made me hesitant to be open about being married to a cis man in queer spaces, and I also felt my identity erased in straight spaces. As I built my online presence as a gender specialist, I kept my personal life private, and people took me at my word that I was queer. It felt good, and I didn't want to lose that! Whenever I made content about being queer or bisexual, I received messages from folks who didn't feel their identity was valid because of their partner. I realized my lack of disclosure was preventing people from seeing someone like them.

So, I shared a video last Pride of me with my spouse that said, "Surprise, I'm queer and married to… this guy! (and still queer)," and it went viral! This led me to co-found bi+ (in)visibility, a community for bi+ folks in straight-presenting relationships, navigating identity together. Now, I get to support people who share my experience and be the one to tell them their identity is valid, regardless of who they are with or their relationship history. It's been really beautiful and healing. Today, I really don't care if people question the authenticity of my identity. I know who I am.

Advocating for Comprehensive Sexuality Education

In earlier chapters, I discussed the ways you can be respectful of someone's sexuality, as well as learning and understanding the role sexuality plays in their life. Now let's examine how you can advocate for your LGBTQIA+ loved ones when they express their sexuality.

One way to advocate is to support comprehensive sex education. According to the International Planned Parenthood Federation,

> Good sexuality education is essential to help young people to prepare for healthy and fulfilling lives. High quality information and comprehensive sexuality education can equip them with the knowledge, skills and attitudes they need to make informed choices now and in the future; to enhance their independence and self-esteem; and to help them to experience their sexuality and relationships in a positive and pleasurable way.[1]

Comprehensive sexuality education does not promote sexual activity; rather, it helps individuals make informed and safe decisions. According to the American College of Obstetricians and Gynecologist (ACOG), "[s]tudies have demonstrated that comprehensive sexuality education programs reduce the rates of sexual activity, sexual risk behaviors (eg, number of partners and unprotected intercourse), sexually transmitted infections, and adolescent pregnancy."[2] Medically accurate and age-appropriate information is an important part of a healthy life. Sexual education programs should be community-based and include information on sexual and gender identities. As ACOG states,

> Programs should not only focus on reproductive development (including abnormalities in development, such as primary ovarian insufficiency and müllerian anomalies), prevention of STIs, and unintended pregnancy, but also teach about forms of sexual expression, healthy sexual and nonsexual relationships, gender identity and sexual orientation and questioning,

communication, recognizing and preventing sexual violence, consent, and decision making.[3]

Those who push for abstinence-based sexual education believe that young adults do not need to be introduced to the facts about sexual activity, for doing so will encourage them to engage in sexual behavior. Teaching young people to repress their sexual feelings, and to feel guilty about sexual behavior, is ineffective. ACOG has found that the opposite is true:

> Comprehensive sexuality education should begin in early childhood and continue through a person's lifespan... The [education]...should include state-specific legal ramifications of sexual behavior and the growing risks of sharing information online. Additionally, programs should cover the variations in sexual expression, including vaginal intercourse, oral sex, anal sex, mutual masturbation, as well as texting and virtual sex.[4]

Comprehensive sexual education helps individuals understand the beauty and diversity of the sexual and gender spectrums as well as how to make informed decisions to protect themselves and their community.

Once Again, With Feeling

The sexual spectrum is beautifully diverse and should be celebrated. As with all humans, LGBTQIA+ individuals only want to express their attraction to and love for another person(s). Policing or legislating who someone can love is discriminatory and dangerous. We should celebrate everyone for who they are and who they choose to build a life with.

If you have a loved one, friend, or coworker who comes out and shares their sexuality with you, remember these two facts: First, they are the same person as they were before. Coming out does not change who a person is—rather it allows you to create a deeper and more impactful relationship with them. Second, celebrate a person who comes out to you. Wear it as a badge of honor, as that person trusts and loves you enough to share their entire self with you.

Coming out is one of the most difficult decisions an LGBTQIA+ individual will ever make. As an ally, help to make it an incredibly joyous process for them.

Summary: Understanding Sexuality

- The Complexities of Sexual Attraction
- The Sexuality "Spectrum"
- Misunderstanding Sexual Activity in the LGBTQIA+ Community
- Heteronormativity
- The Sexual Spectrum is Fluid
- Seeking a Greater Understanding of Sexuality
- Advocating for Comprehensive Sexuality Education
- Once Again, With Feeling

7. Pronouns and Lived Names

"If I wait for someone else to validate my existence, it will mean that I'm shortchanging myself." —Zanele Muholi, South African artist and activist

In today's society, many people struggle to understand how to properly refer to LGBTQIA+ individuals. Part of being an ally is to know how to correctly refer to and address someone when using their name and pronouns. The pronouns and name(s) an individual uses are a reflection of their lived identity. This chapter will give you tools to help you become comfortable with pronouns and lived names.

Pronouns

In the grammatical sense, pronouns are parts of speech used to designate a person or thing. "I," "you," "it," "he," "she," "we," and "they," have traditionally been used in English to separate objects ("it") from humans, and to classify humans by singular ("I," "he," "she") or plural ("we," "they.") Traditionally, pronouns also divided human beings into binary categories, according to their assigned sex at birth ("he" or "she.")

The LBGTQIA+ community challenges traditional English pronoun usage by insisting that pronouns should not have a gender or singular/plural designation. Pronouns' traditional role of replacing a person(s) in a sentence ("He is here" instead of "John is here") should be maintained, but the gender and singular/plural binaries should be removed ("They are here" instead of "John is here.") This new pronoun usage is not a preference or a choice, but a lived reality, leading to the use of the term, "lived pronouns."

It should be understood that the pronouns a person uses are the ones you should use when addressing or referring to them. Small changes in language can really make a huge difference in people's lives—and can even be life saving!

Here are some of the most frequently asked questions about lived pronouns.

Why Focus On Pronouns?

You can't always tell someone's gender by looking at them. Using their correct personal pronouns is respectful and creates an inclusive environment. One of the easiest ways to cause someone harm is by misgendering them by intentionally using the incorrect pronouns. Would you want to be addressed by an incorrect gender?

Who Might Use Gender Neutral Pronouns?

People who may not identify as strictly a woman or a man, such as nonbinary. It may also be good to use neutral pronouns when you do not know what the person prefers. Once again, lived pronouns are not tied to certain genders. A person of any gender can use any pronoun that they feel accurately refers to who they are as a person.

What Are Some Examples Of Gender-Neutral Pronouns, More Commonly Referred To As "Neopronouns"?

There are many, but here are some examples: they, them, theirs; xe, xir, xirs; ze, zir, zirs.

Some people do not use pronouns at all, feeling that they misgender them completely. In this case, use the person's name rather than a pronoun.

Is The Singular "They" Grammatically Correct?

This is probably the most highly debated topic, with many

opponents to transgender rights stating that "they" is a "made up"pronoun that can only be used in the plural. The short answer is, YES! In 2019, the *Washington Post* style guide, the *Merriam-Webster Dictionary*, and the *Oxford Dictionary* all recognized the singular "they" as a gender-neutral pronoun.[1] In fact, the singular "they" was used as early as 1375 CE, where it appears in the medieval romantic poem "William and the Werewolf." Since then, "they"has typically only been used to refer to a single person when their gender is unknown. ("Someone left their wallet on the table.")

Using the singular "they" really isn't difficult! Simply replace "he" and "she" with "they", "them," or "theirs." You do not need to change any other parts of the language in your sentence in order to be inclusive!

Why Are Gender Neutral/Gender Inclusive Pronouns Important?

Using someone's pronouns accurately shows respect and acceptance.

Are Pronouns A Choice?

Just like an individual's sexuality and gender, pronouns are not a choice, but a tool for accurately referring to and referencing a person and their gender(s).

Do People Change Pronouns Over Time?

Yes, in some cases. For transgender individuals, the journey to understanding their gender identity is a long process, and can change along the way. A person might start out using one set of pronouns, only to realize that other pronouns better align with their gender. In instances like this, the best way to be respectful is to ask that person what pronouns they prefer.

Who Should I Ask About Their Pronouns?

Ideally everyone. Asking people about their pronouns is an

excellent practice that doesn't single out non-gender conforming, trans, genderfluid, or other gender minorities.

How Do I Ask Which Pronouns To Use When Speaking With Or About Someone?

If possible, introduce yourself first. For example, "Hi, my name is Kat and my pronouns are they, them and their. How would you like me to refer to you?" This is the easiest way to break the ice and show that you are respectful of lived pronouns.

If you already know the person and want to check what pronouns to use, this example would work:. "Hello, Jen! I wanted to ask what pronouns you'd like me to use when referring to you?"

What If I Ask Someone Their Pronouns And They Ask Why?

Give them an example, such as: "Someone with the name Elizabeth may go by Liz or Beth, and I just want to make sure I use the right one with you to show my respect."

How Can I Support Someone With Multiple Pronouns?

Summer Bedard (she/he) was quoted by Wren Sanders (she/they) in an article for *Them* as saying that, "[p]eople who use multiple pronouns are showcasing the complexity of their identity to the world, and I think that's really beautiful, because it shows others that it's okay to embrace all the many sides of yourself at once."[2]

Gently asking if someone uses one set of pronouns in particular contexts is also good, because some folks may feel affirmed through using multiple sets simultaneously—i.e., "He/They went to the store." This is a less common preference, so it's probably safest to ask in advance about this approach. Whatever answer you get, don't press if it's not totally clear to you—the reasons an individual uses one set versus another in certain situations can be very personal.

What If I Accidentally Use The Wrong Pronouns For Someone?

Apologize briefly, use the correct pronoun, and move on. We are all human and make mistakes. If the person corrects you, simply say, "thank you for correcting me." You are accepting your mistake and taking ownership for making it, even if it was unintentional. By doing this, you allow the person who was misgendered to feel respected.

What If I Observe Someone Using The Wrong Pronouns?

If appropriate, gently correct the speaker using the individual's correct pronouns: "Oh, you mean when she went to the store."

If a misgendered person does not correct the incorrect use of their pronouns, it is not okay to misgender that person. It likely means that the person ignored the misgendering for safety reasons.

I am misgendered a lot—typically, several times a day. Some people continue to refer to me with male pronouns—he, him, or sir,—even though I have breasts and dress in very feminine attire. Sometimes I will correct the person and explain that my pronouns are they/she; other times, I won't say anything.. Why don't I stand up for myself and state my gender in all situations? The short answer is that it is not my job to educate everyone. I get tired of having to explain my gender and my pronouns. It is not the responsibility of an LGBTQIA+ person to educate the public—it is on the public to educate themselves. Sometimes, I stay quiet for safety. I have had several encounters with people who have become hostile and have berated me for standing up for myself. Unfortunately, this is extremely common. Transgender individuals have to quickly determine whether or not they will be safe if they correct someone who misgenders them.

Misgendering is one of the greatest issues a transgender individual deals with, and one of the common triggers for gender dysphoria, depression, anxiety, and suicide. As an ally, one of the best things you can do is to correct misgendering when you see it, and check in with the person who was misgendered.

What If Someone Is Hesitant To Share Their Pronouns?

Introduce yourself with your own pronouns: "Hi, I'm John, and my pronouns are they/them/theirs." This allows the other person to share theirs if they wish, but doesn't force them to do so. Sometimes people are fearful of disclosing their pronouns due to previous hostile responses. Provide a safe space for them to do so, if possible.

How Else Can I Be Inclusive Of Someone's Pronouns?

Below are some incredibly simple ways you can show your respect and inclusiveness of pronoun usage.

> Add your pronouns to your email signature. Look at mine as an example.
> Mx. NV Gay
> Photographer, Activist, Educator, Writer
> (They/She)
>
> Add your pronouns on name tags:
> Jimmy Smith
> (He/Him/His)

These inclusive practices make a huge difference in an LGBTQIA+ person's life. Speaking as a transgender person, when I see someone displaying their pronouns, it puts me at ease and tells me that I am safe with that individual. This in turn will allow the person to open up and be honest with you, rather than holding back information for safety concerns. This is extremely important in professional settings, and in particular, in medicine, as most transgender individuals do not feel safe when receiving medical care due to constant misgendering by practitioners.

Other Important Aspects Of Lived Pronouns

Len Meyer of Planned Parenthood of Illinois writes that, "[p]ronoun usage is just one step in changing language and supporting those living outside of the binary. It's also important to remember that other gendered terms must also be put into perspective when someone changes their pronouns."[3] Language such as how to refer to someone is typically gendered; for example, daughter, son, brother, sister, husband, wife, mother, father, niece, nephew, etc. It could be replaced with non-gender language such as child, parent, spouse, sibling, nibling, etc. Using these non-gendered labels is more inclusive of all people, no matter their gender.

A post on the Community Commons Beyond Inclusion blog states that

> According to a recent study on pronoun use, TGNB youth whose pronouns were respected by all or most of the people in their lives attempted suicide at half the rate of those whose pronouns were not respected. When compared with TGNB youth who aren't able to use their chosen name and associated pronouns in any context, young people who can safely use their chosen name in all four key contexts (school, home, work and with friends) experience a significant improvement in health outcomes, including:
>> 71% fewer symptoms of severe depression
>> 34% decrease in reported thoughts of suicide
>> 65% decrease in suicidal attempts[4]

Lived Names

Being respectful of a person's lived name is just as important as using their correct pronouns. A lived name, often referred to as a "chosen name," is one used by an individual rather than their legal name. A lived name may reflect gender identity, a nickname, an Americanized version of a name from another culture, or a means of distinguishing oneself from someone with a similar name. Many people in the United States use their middle name rather than a first name, or a shortened version of their legal name, such as "Bob" instead of "Robert." For transgender individuals, lived names are a reflection of their true self. Many trans people are uncomfortable with the names given to them at birth —their "dead names"—and thus turn to a lived name.

Addressing a person by their lived name, rather than insisting on using their legal (dead) name, is important. Some individuals might not have legally changed their name due to the time, cost, and complicated requirements of the process. All people want to be addressed by their correct name! Using a person's chosen name is a simple way to honor who they are.

Here are a few ways to become comfortable with lived names.

Ask the person their name or what they'd like to be called, just as you might ask someone their nickname.

Use that name for them in all situations.

Never ask a person to reveal their dead name to you.

If you use the wrong name by mistake, correct yourself.

Some professional situations, such as medical settings, will require individuals to use a legal name for purposes of documentation. Most transgender individuals understand and accept this, but they still wish to be addressed by their lived names during personal interactions. In these situations, you should ask the person their lived name and pronouns, and then only refer to them in that way. This will save everyone from hurt and confusion.

Imagine the following scenario.

THE QUEER ALLIES BIBLE

A transgender woman whose lived name is "Allie" must use her legal name, "Jonathan," when filling out forms in a doctor's office. The nurse calls for "Jonathan" shortly afterward. This forces her to respond to a dead name. It also reveals private information about her gender identity to strangers. Above all, it makes her feel very unsafe and distrustful of the medical staff.. It would have been very easy for the person taking the documentation to have informed the staff of "Allie's" lived name. Simple acts like this are profoundly important to LGBTQIA+ individuals.

Being an LGBTQIA+ ally means being respectful of a person's pronouns and name, even if you don't understand their choices. It's okay if you happen to slip up and make a mistake from time to time; we all do. When mistakes happen, take ownership and correct it. When you observe a person being misgendered or referred to incorrectly, step in and correct the speaker. Make these practices a normal part of your personal and professional life, as you never know when you will interact with an LGBTQIA+ individual.

Summary: Pronouns and Lived Names

- Pronouns
- FAQ About Lived Pronouns
- Other Important Aspects of Lived Pronouns
- Lived Names

PART TWO:
HOW TO BE AN ALLY

8. Responding To Anti-LGBTQIA+ Rhetoric and Attitudes

"Always remember, we are the new ancestors; so act accordingly."
—Te D. DeMornay, Mx., Trans New Mexico 2024 of the White Mountain Apache and San Carlos Apache Tribes

Members of the LGBTQIA+ community receive negativity on a daily basis, from demeaning and misinformed comments, to being misgendered, to facing open hostility and targeted violence. When I talk about the difficulties I've experienced as a transgender individual, most people respond by saying that they're "sorry." Beyond expressing your sympathy, you can be an effective and compassionate ally by asking yourself what you can do to make sure no LGBTQIA+ individual faces discriminatory and harmful practices. One of the hardest parts of being an ally is learning how to defend the LGBTQIA+ community in conversations with other people. Many people recognize when transphobic and homophobic comments are made, but are unsure of how to counter them.

Here, I will list the types of comments that you will likely hear in regards to the LGBTQIA+ community, and offer you ways to address them. Be aware that a person who makes an anti-LGBTQIA+ comment may react with hostility to being corrected. Unfortunately, this is a reality that many LGBTQIA+ people encounter when they stand up for themselves. Sometimes it is beneficial to address negative comments privately with the person rather than calling them out in the moment. Be mindful of the situation and make sure that you are keeping yourself safe.

Consider the following comments and suggested responses:

"Sexuality Is A Choice."

The idea that an individual can choose whether or not to be gay has persisted for decades. In reality, sexuality is not a choice, but an innate aspect of a person's identity. We are attracted to who we are attracted to, and there is nothing wrong with that.

As a response, you can say something like, "You are right, there is a choice in being queer. The choice is to accept the truth about who that person is and stop adhering to a hetronormative narrative that causes many people to experience self-loathing and mental anguish. They did not choose to be sexually attracted to _____, but they did choose to be free."

"Kids Raised By Queer Parents Will Become Queer Themselves."

No one chooses their sexual or gender identity, regardless of their parents' sexuality. Instead, people discover their identity through lived experiences and self-realization. Young people are capable of making decisions for themselves, and will come to a natural understanding of their gender and sexual identity.

As a response, you can say, "A child's gender or sexual identity is not influenced by the identity of their parents. We certainly learn from our parents and are influenced by their opinions, but our own gender or sexual identity cannot be learned or taught."

"Children Need A Stable Home With A Mom And A Dad."

No study has found any evidence to prove that households with LGBTQIA+ parents are inherently unstable. Thus, there is no basis to believe that families containing two moms, two dads, etc., are better or worse than traditional homes with a mother and a father.[1] With nearly 400,000 children in the foster care system in the United States, there is an undeniable need for LGBTQIA+ parents.

As a response, you can say something such as, "LGBTQIA+

individuals deserve to raise a family, just as any other person does. There is nothing to prove that LGBTQIA+ individuals are less unfit to raise a child than a straight person."

"You Cannot Be A Boy Unless You Were Born With A Penis." "You Cannot Be A Girl Unless You Were Born With A Vagina."

Social tradition long held that gender was connected to the sex a person was assigned at birth. Today, research shows that a person's gender is an outward expression of their self-understanding, and is not determined by their sexual anatomy. Simply put, your brain determines your gender, not your body parts.

As a response, you can say that, "If someone understands themselves to be a girl/boy/nonbinary/etc., then we should respect that. They understand their body, mind, and soul far better than we do. How they feel about themselves is much more important than their body parts."

"Children Are Too Young To Receive Gender-Affirming Care."

Gender-affirming medical care for minors has been the focus of recent legislation across this country, with many states making such care illegal. In reality, minor children only receive gender-affirming surgeries when they are medically necessary, generally after years of medical care.

We should carefully consider whether the government should have a say in a family's medical decisions. Parents, medical practitioners, and patients should be the only people involved in decisions regarding a transgender child's gender-affirming care. Delaying treatment subjects an individual to dysphoria, mental anguish, and depression. Gender-affirming care is life-saving care.

As a response, you can say, "Children go through periods of gender exploration like they go through clothing styles. Allowing a child to explore their understanding of gender is natural and safe. Children typically do not receive any permanent treatments regarding their gender until after they reach the age of eighteen, and after years of therapy and medical observation."

"Queer People Are Groomers."

Homophobic people have long claimed that LGBTQIA+ individuals are pedophiles, preying on youth in an attempt to "convert" them into "queers." This is not only untrue, but it dehumanizes the LGBTQIA+ community and perpetuates hate and discrimination towards it.

As a response, say something like, "LGBTQIA+ individuals have no desire to 'convert' your children. They only want to live safe and productive lives."

"Holy Matrimony Can Only Occur Between A Man And A Woman."

This idea is based on traditional religious beliefs, as well as the notion that humanity's purpose is to procreate. The truth is that marriage is defined as a consenting relationship between adults. Opponents of marriage equality state that there needs to be a line drawn because if not, a person could "marry" anyone or anything. I have heard absurdities such as, "If we allow gay marriage, what's next—a man marrying his dog?" This "slippery slope" argument justifies discrimination and invalidates loving, committed relationships between LGBTQIA+ adults.

As a response, you can say something such as, "Mutual love and respect between consenting adults are what makes a marriage, not an obligation to reproduce."

"Being Queer Is A Sin."

Many people use religious texts and claims of faith to justify negative acts towards the LGTBQIA+ community. Sadly, religion can be used to excuse many forms of discrimination. Instead of using spiritual texts and messages to justify exclusionary practices, we should use these core beliefs to spread love and acceptance for all. See the "Religion and the

LGTBQIA+ Community" chapter for a greater discussion of this issue.

As a response, try, "Religion is meant to spread a message of inclusion, love, and acceptance for all. You do not have to agree with LGBTQIA+ identities, but you need to accept them and treat all people with respect and dignity."

"Transgenderism Is An Ideology, Not An Identity."

This statement is embraced by anti-trans extremists who seek to dehumanize transgender individuals by questioning the validity of their identity. GLAAD explains that "[t]he term 'transgenderism' was notably weaponized in a vicious March 2023 speech by right-wing extremist Michael Knowles at CPAC, the Conservative Political Action Conference, where Knowles [stated] that 'For the good of society … transgenderism must be eradicated from public life entirely.' Knowles posted versions of the speech on YouTube, as well as variations of the same rhetoric on his other social media accounts, while disingenuously asserting that his genocidal call was not genocidal."[2]

As a response, say something like, "Ideas like this dehumanize transgender individuals. Make an effort to get to know transgender individuals and learn from them."

"Dating A Trans-Femme Or Trans-Masc Person Makes You Gay."

This homophobic and transphobic claim comes from the heteronormative and cisnormative belief that transwomen are not women and transmen are not men. Simply, transwomen are women and transmen are men. How a person was identified at birth does not define who they are.

As a response, you can say something such as, "A person's gender is not defined by their body parts, but by their understanding of their individual soul and spirit. A woman who identifies as a woman is just that, a woman. Therefore a cisgender man dating a transwoman is simply a man dating a woman, and therefore not a homosexual."

"LGB Without The T" (The Rejection Of Transgender Members Of The LGBTQIA+ Community.)

Some people who adhere to this cisnormative narrative believe that transgender people make acceptance of LGB people more difficult. When someone identifies only within the sexuality aspect of their identity, they can often blend into society more easily and therefore experience less discrimination. Some LGB people believe that gender diversity has led to an increase in hostility toward all LGBTQIA+ people.

The Trans-Exclusionary Radical Feminists, known as TERFs, insist that transgender women are men, not women. These individuals believe that general hostility against transgender women ultimately prevents all women from gaining equality. Internet posts by author J.K. Rowling has contributed to this argument.

As a response, you can say something such as, "Gender and sexual identity are complex. They cannot be invalidated by anyone. Transgender people have existed throughout history and have played a role in all of the modern liberation movements, including the fight for Women's Suffrage and LGBTQIA+ equality."

"Bisexuality/Pansexuality Is A Phase."

Just as someone's gender identity is uniquely theirs, so to is their sexuality. Yes, a bisexual woman might end up being in a relationship with a man, but that does not invalidate her bisexuality. Attraction is complex and resists categorization. A person's sexuality is a private matter. Understand it, accept it, and affirm it!

Bisexual and pansexual individuals often face discrimination from people who see them as "invalid" unless they are in a relationship with someone of a different gender. Many bisexual and pansexual individuals face criticism if they are engaged in heteronormative relationships. Again, sexuality is private.

As a response, say, "A bisexual person is not defined by their current relationship or by anyone outside that relationship."

Here is an incredible quote from bisexual activit Robyn Ochs: "I call myself bisexual because I acknowledge that I have in myself the potential to be attracted—romantically and/or sexually—to people of more than one sex and/or gender, not necessarily at the same time, not necessarily in the same way, and not necessarily to the same degree."[3]

"LGBTQIA+ People Aren't Mistreated Where I Live."

Mistreatment or harassment of the LGBTQIA+ community is often not widely publicized, especially in rural areas. Oftentimes, LGBTQIA+ individuals who have been mistreated or harassed are afraid of coming forward and speaking up. While social media platforms have given each person a greater voice, many LGBTQIA+ voices are often suppressed in order to promote content that is considered more valuable by the platform.

In reality, violence against the LGBTQIA+ community continues to rise, as "LGBT people are nearly four times more likely than non-LGBT people to experience violent victimization, including rape, sexual assault, and aggravated or simple assault. In addition, LGBT people are more likely to experience violence both by someone well-known to the victim and at the hands of a stranger."[4]

As a response, consider saying something such as: "LGBTQ-IA+ individuals are four times more likely to face mistreatment or harassment because of their identity than non-LGBTQIA+ individuals. Just because you don't hear about it doesn't mean that it doesn't happen. Too often, LGBTQIA+ individuals are afraid to report mistreatment or harassment due to the negative repercussions they face when they do come forward."

"Trans People Are Not Really Trans, They're Just Following A Trend."

This idea has grown more common as more transgender individuals, like Dylan Mulvanney, who used TikTok to gain fame for her "Days of Girlhood" series, use social media platforms to gain visibility. To repeat, transgender individuals have existed throughout history. Transitioning genders is not a simple process. It often leads to years of extreme stress and anxiety. Some claim transgender athletes like Lia Thomas transitioned because she could not "win" in the male divisions of competitive swimming. But who would choose to become the target of all of the hate and discrimination transgender individuals face? Who would go through hormone replacement therapy just to win a race?

As a response, you can say something such as: "No one in their right mind would choose to be transgender unless they actually were transgender. To go through all of the external and internal changes to their bodies, as well as the discrimination and hate, would not be worth it unless they were actually transgender. The only reason for a person to transition genders is because they are transgender, not because they want their fifteen minutes of fame."

"All Transgender People Are Autistic."

Recent research suggests that members of the LGBTQIA+ community have higher levels of autism and other so-called "mental and physical disabilities." According to the Autism Research Institute, "[c]ontemporary research on the intersection of autism, sexuality, and gender identity asserts that autistic individuals are more likely to identify as LGBTQIA+ than the neurotypical population. Similarly, the prevalence of autism is higher among transgender people than cisgender individuals."[5] Despite these findings, autism and other neurodivergent conditions are not an automatic feature of LGBTQIA+ identities. LGBTQIA+ people should never be mistreated due to the expectation that they are neurodivergent.

As a response, you can say something such as, "Every person should be treated with empathy, and should never be mistreated due to an expectation that they are neurodivergent."

"Transgender Is A Fetish / Kink."

Within the fetish and kink communities, transgender identities do exist, but are often mistaken for fetish identities such as "sissy," "forced feminization," and more. The key is to not confuse transgender identities with fetishes. "Kinks" are described as non-conventional sexual practices, concepts or fantasies, while "fetishes" are defined as a sexual excitement towards an object, non-sexual organ of the body, or taboo actions.[6] There are many fetishes and kinks. and it needs to be stated that they are completely normal and valid so long as all partners are consenting. There may be overlap between fetishes and gender or sexual identity. For example, some who engage in a forced feminization fetish may be transgender, and others may not be. Individuals within the LGBTQIA+ community engage in fetishes as well as porn, but that does not make their gender identity or sexuality invalid.

As a response, you can say something such as, "Fetishes and kinks are completely normal sexual activity and do not define a person's gender identity or sexuality. Yes, some LGBTQIA+ individuals engage in fetishes, but that does not define or invalidate their identity."

As an ally, humanizing LGBTQIA+ individuals when responding to the above statements and comments is vital. Challenge people who make some of these comments to actually get to know LGBTQIA+ individuals. Ask them not to repeat their anti-LGBTQIA+ rhetoric. Tell them that people who identify as LGBTQIA+ do so because that is who they are.

Narratives challenging LGBTQIA+ people's identity exist because far too many people don't understand genders and sexual identities different from their own. While the old adage, walk a mile in someone else's shoes, is a great way to think, you cannot just simply walk a mile in an LGBTQIA+ individual's shoes. You instead must believe their identity, accept that they are who they say they are, and then affirm them for who they are.

Misgendering and Using Dead Names

Misgendering a person by using the wrong pronouns, or referring to them by their dead name, might not seem particularly negative or hurtful, especially in comparison to some of the remarks we have just examined. These things typically go unchecked, as most people write them off as a mistake without realizing they might have been done intentionally. Misgendering and using dead names often occur when LGBTQIA+ individuals are not present. Still, they need to be corrected.

In some instances, an LGBTQIA+ person may be publicly misgendered in their presence, and they don't correct the person misgendering them—as I shared in the previous chapter that I sometimes do myself, because I get exhausted from always having to correct people, or for safety reasons. Too often, people become mean, and even violent, when they are corrected, and this can be terrifying. There are hundreds of documented cases where LGBTQIA+ people are attacked for standing up for themselves.

How then should you react as an ally when someone is misgendered? Engage the person who is saying such things in a polite manner. You can explain to them, "Oh hey, just so you know, their pronouns are they/them, and their name is Casey." Keep it simple and direct. If possible, politely encourage the person to correct their speech in the future. Most of the time, they will apologize and that will be the end of it. In cases where the person becomes aggressive or defensive, *politely* reiterate the correction—no one wins when the situation escalates to an argument. Some people will absolutely refuse to be corrected, and nothing will change their minds. If this happens in the workplace or in a school setting, report them to human resources or the administration and let the authorities handle the situation further. Do not play the role of "hero"—just be a loving and accepting ally.

Be sure to check in on the LGBTQIA+ person that has to deal with being misgendered. Make sure they are okay, feel safe, and ask what you can to help them. Seeing that they are not alone and that their allies truly care enough to stand up for them makes an incredible difference.

Show Your Values!

Beyond your personal relationship, advocating for the LGBTQIA+ people in your life also means fighting policies that negatively impact the community. You don't have to march on the front lines of protests, or speak in opposition to legislation at your state house—activism can be as simple as displaying a sign at your residence declaring that you're an ally. When Donald Trump was elected president the first time, many people placed signs in their yards stating things such as "Science is Real," "Love is Love," and "Women's Rights Are Human Rights." These messages gave hope to victims of discrimination. The sight of a rainbow flag signals that I'm in a place where I don't have to worry about being attacked for simply being myself. It gives me joy to know that there are those in the world who want to see marginalized individuals thrive.

Vote Your Beliefs!

An electorate that supports LGBTQIA+ rights is critical. While voter turnout for local and midterm elections is incredibly low, who sits on school boards, library boards, and on city councils has a huge impact on community life. Many local officials across the country are pushing an anti-LGBTQIA agenda based on misinformation and unfounded fear. Currently, forty-nine states have proposed anti-LGBTQIA+ policies and legislation, most of which occurs at the local level.[7]

As a result, getting out and voting for local officials who support LGBTQIA+ rights is crucial. If you are unsure about a candidate's position, turn to organizations like The Victory Fund, which endorses officials at all levels of government who are fighting for and supporting the LGBTQIA+ community.

Become An Educated Ally

Learning about anti-LGBTQIA+ issues on your own so that your coworkers, friends, or loved ones don't have to teach you is a key part of being a great ally and advocate. There are so many credible organizations that can offer answers to your LGBTQIA+ questions. You can also reach out to your local LGBTQ community center, as they have programs and events geared towards creating community and providing education.

Becoming an educated ally will help you understand LGBTQIA+ identities and orientations, as well as the challenges LGBTQIA+ individuals experience on a regular basis. Read about the history of the Gay Rights Movement. The adage that history repeats itself is very true. This is not the first time that LGBTQIA+ rights have been under attack, nor will not be the last.

Also understand also that the experiences of an LGBTQIA+ person may be very different from those of other marginalized communities. Do not invalidate the experiences of LGBTQIA+ people by claiming you "know what they are going through." Instead, listen to them. Help them in the healing process. Never belittle them or say that their experiences were "not that bad."

The Importance Of Reclaimed Words
Queer
Many words have historically specifically been used to promote hatred and discrimination against the LGBTQIA+ community.

"Queer" is one such word. Before the twentieth century, "queer" was defined as something strange, odd, peculiar, or eccentric. Later, it became common to describe someone who identified within the LGBTQIA+ community as "queer." It was used to shame someone—especially people who were not actually LGBTQIA+—by ridiculing them for seeming to be outside of the heterosexual gender binary.

Recently, many in the LGBTQIA+ community have "reclaimed" the word and now use it to demonstrate power, unity, and pride in our identity—and in the title of this book! Not everyone agrees, however. Some members of the LGBTQIA+ community, especially those from older generations, still see this word as disrespectful and hurtful.

So, as an ally, is it acceptable to use the word "queer" when describing an LGBTQIA+ person? The answer is yes—provided you have been given permission from the person to use it. If you are a cisgender heterosexual ally, you should only describe specific individuals as "queer" after they've allowed you to use the term. Keep in mind that having the permission of one person does not grant you permission to describe everyone in the community as "queer." Be aware that people have had a range of experiences with the word, and in some instances, it has been the cause of serious trauma. While the term has been reclaimed, it should still be used with caution and respect.

Transexual

Similarly, there is much debate within the trans community as to whether the identity "transsexual" should still be used to define a trans person. People from older generations used "transsexual" to identify themselves, understanding that they were transitioning their sex through medical and social practices. To them, this process was understood to be the only way to validly transition. Today, we understand transitioning very differently. So the question remains, should the identity "transsexual" be used? In my opinion, the answer is yes, as "transexual" is just another term to help individuals understand their identity. Being transexual is not any more valid than being transgender; rather, it is just another means of understanding of who that person is. It is important to understand how each person identifies themselves, and respect the way in which they do so. The only person who can validly understand and determine a gender or sexual identity is that person.

Instead of focusing on terms, labels, and identities, I would advise you to focus on the individual. You will never be disrespectful if you refer to someone by their lived name or nickname, rather than using a term to refer to that person. Saying, "Hey queer," could be completely fine with a close friend, but would likely be incredibly insensitive and disrespectful to a stranger. It is also inappropriate to refer to someone by their gender, sexual, racial, or religious identity, as it only perpetuates the stereotypes and discrimination surrounding these labels. While individuality and membership in multiple communities ("intersectionality") is important to recognize, we do not need to focus on using a person's identity in order to refer to them.

How to Handle Hate

I am often asked, "How do you combat all of the hate towards the LGBTQIA+ community?"

This is an excellent question, and it took me a while to develop an answer. It was only after I examined my past and how I myself used to behave towards the LGBTQIA+ community that I began to understand why people can be so hateful.

In general, hate towards an individual or community does not just appear, but is born through a person's lived experiences. Sometimes hate is learned—passed down from generation to generation. People learn behaviors and negative feelings from their parents, religious institutions, or even from their teachers. Other times, hate comes from trauma, where an individual expresses hatred towards others because of something they hate about themself, or something they experienced.

Let's begin with learned hate. This comes from message such as "we do not like a person or a community because they…" These kinds of statements can be difficult to refute, for they are typically instilled in people from a very young age. This hatred seems illogical, unfounded, and very threatening to its victims. Attempts to reason with its proponents are usually dismissed. Too often, people who say these things are dismissed or called ignorant. This only deepens their hatred. You cannot fight hate with hate; you have to combat it by giving these individuals the same love that you would like to receive in return. This can be extremely hard, and can seem like it's not working. It will take time and patience.

Engaging in calm conversation with these individuals can help. Shouting facts at them will never work, but sitting down and having an honest conversation might. Talk to them and ask about their beliefs, and then share your experiences. A lot of the time these people have never had a real conversation with an individual of the group they "hate." Share your experiences and engage with them about theirs. Treating others the way you want to be treated is always a strong strategy in overcoming hatred.

Hate can also be trauma-related or a result of self-hatred. This happens for many reasons, and is extremely difficult to overcome until you get to the heart of the problem. Let me give you two examples. First, when I was closeted, I was extremely hateful towards the LGBTQIA+ community. While I had learned some of this hate from my upbringing and from lessons at church, my hate was truly born from the self-hatred of my sense of gender. I was so confused and lost in my understanding of self that I felt that I had to project the hyper-masculine heterosexual narrative to make sure that others did not see me as "feminine" or homosexual—also due to my last name, "Gay"—and I projected that narrative on others. I was truly horrible to LGBTQIA+ individuals, as I needed to project hatred on them to make sure I

140

would remain hidden.

The second example involves a student of mine when I was a middle school teacher. This student was extremely hateful toward police officers, believing that they were only out to get them. This student's hatred was deep and personal, and only after many conversations did I discover that it was born from a traumatic experience: when this student was young, the police raided his house and took his father away in handcuffs. He was unaware of any crimes his father might have committed, so what he retained was the fear he had experienced.

What I hope you understand is that hate can be seen as completely valid to a person, as they are using their pain to cover up the traumatic experience or self-hatred that shaped them. I am not saying that this is okay—what I am saying is that you have to be empathetic to people who are expressing hatred to cover up something deep inside. These people need to heal and deal with the issues that drive them to hate. They need your love and empathy.

Finally, some people project hate just to be hateful. Unfortunately, this is not something that you are going to be able to change. You are unlikely to overcome their hostility, even with patience, kindness, or attempts to educate them. If this is the case, it is better to protect yourself and move on.

When you put all of the above together, you'll begin to become an ally to the LGBTQIA+ community. Remember to listen to individuals. Honor their pronouns and lived names. Stand up for them, even when they're not present. Use affirming words and respect their confidentiality. Speak up when anti-LGBTQIA+ jokes or derisive comments are made. Engage in public—and private—demonstrations of activism, and vote for candidates who support the LGBTQIA+ community. Rember that allies are critical in bringing positive and affirming change for all the LGBTQIA+ community.

Summary: Responding To Anti-LGBTQIA+ Rhetoric and Attitudes

- Responding to Anti-LGBTQIA+ Remarks and Statements
- Anti-LGBTQIA+ Speech
- "Sexuality is a Choice."
- "Kids raised by queer parents will become queer themselves."
- "Children need a stable home with a Mom and a Dad"
- "You cannot be a boy unless you were born with a penis." "You cannot be a girl unless you were born with a vagina."
- "Children are too young to receive gender-affirming care."
- "Queer people are groomers."
- "Queers only want to convert our children."
- "Holy Matrimony can only occur between a man and a woman."
- "Being queer is a sin."
- "Transgenderism is an ideology, not an identity."
- "Dating a trans-femme or trans-masc person makes you gay."
- "LGB without the T"
- "Bisexaulity/Pansexuality is a phase."
- "LGBTQIA+ people aren't mistreated in my area."

- "Trans people are not really trans, they're just following a trend."
- "All transgender people are autistic."
- "Transgender is a fetish / kink."
- Misgendering and Using Dead Names.
- Show Your Values!
- Vote your beliefs!
- The Importance of Reclaimed Words
- How to Handle Hate

9. Intersectionality and Creating Safe Spaces

"A little Consideration, a little Thought for Others, makes all the difference."—Eeyore, *Winnie-the-Pooh*

What is Intersectionality?

One way to be an ally to the LGBTQIA+ community is to understand your points of intersection with others, and to determine how you can use those common realities to uplift and fight for marginalized individuals. This process is known as "intersectionality," which can be defined in more detail as

> ...an analytic framework that addresses how interlocking systems of power impact those who are most marginalized in society. Taking an intersectional approach means looking beyond a person's individual identities and focusing on the points of intersection that their multiple identities create. The term was coined by black feminist and legal scholar Kimberle Crenshaw to describe how individuals with multiple marginalized identities can experience multiple and unique forms of discrimination that cannot be conceptualized separately.[1]

Consider what makes up your identity—your race, ethnicity, sex, gender identity, religion, level of education, economic class, even your age. Most people understand these aspects of themselves, but rarely think about how others' identities are similar—or "intersectional"—with theirs. If you are cisgender, for example, you might never have thought about the challenges faced by those who identify differently.

Understanding the ways your life shares intersectional points with other individuals will help you see how they are marginalized. Instead of focusing on the ways we are different, look at the natural similarities that exist between us—then consider how much less challenging life is for heterosexual cisgender people. Fitting comfortably inside the heteronormative gender binary offers a person many privileges which can be used to benefit others.

As an ally, you can help create safe spaces and amplify marginalized voices by giving LGBTQIA+ people the opportunity to share their knowledge and experiences. Victoria Nguyen, a student at the Eccles School of Business at the University of Utah, writes that, "[m]arginalized community members bring different perspectives than their relatively more privileged peers, shedding light on specific issues associated with living under systemic oppression. The single story creates stereotypes, but stereotypes do not provide the full story."[2]

"Single story" refers to the danger of only listening to one representative of a marginalized community when it is important to understand that all members of that community are not the same. For example, my lived experiences as a transgender lesbian are not the same as those of an asexual person. While we both identify within the LGBTQIA+ umbrella, our experiences are vastly different. "Listening to marginalized voices," Nguyen continues, "allows for the single story to develop into the full story. Not only does it decrease social exclusion but allows for constructive ideas for improving organizational processes and functions to reach decision-makers. Prioritizing all voices at all organizational levels is critical to achieving better decision-making practices, increased creativity, and improved inclusion."[3]

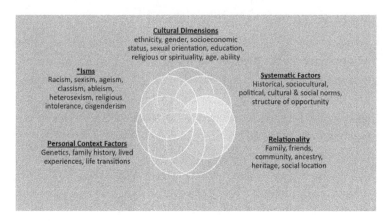

The above graphic illustrates the concept of intersectionality. Thinking about the ways the circles intersect shows us how people who may appear to be very different actually share many similarities. If you are granted social privileges because you belong to mainstream society, you may still share a great deal with those who are marginalized. Focus on ways of supporting others, rather than on the ways that your ideas, lives, and worldview are different. Remember that our society offers unearned privilege to some based on their race, sex, and socio-economic status. Those who lack privilege may never have the opportunity to be heard, to be treated with respect, or to be given the chance to succeed. True "equity" is impossible until we acknowledge that lived experiences are far more complex than what may be indicated by one's appearance, or what's written on a resume. We respect people by listening to their voices and learning about their challenges, then asking what we can do to help.

Equity vs. Equality

Many people misunderstand the distinction between equity and equality. *Equality* means that each individual or community is given the same resources and opportunities; *equity* recognizes that each person has different circumstances and requires different accommodations and opportunities in order to reach an outcome equal to those with more privilege. Equality and equity are often confused, as people believe that if everyone is given the same resources, they will have equal opportunities. This is not true.

Consider this example: suppose you gave two people, one poor and one rich, the equal sum of $1,000. The poor person might immediately spend the money on basic needs, such as food and housing, while the rich person, whose basic needs are already met, might choose to invest it, increasing its worth. The poor person did nothing wrong—they used the money to survive. The rich person, however, had the privilege of using the money to increase their wealth. The "equal" sum of $1,000 did not result in "equal" opportunity for the poor person.

Equity would dictate that you give a much larger sum of money to the poor person and a much smaller sum to the rich person. This would allow the poor person to overcome challenges that the rich person does not have to face. Ideally, with the equitable allocation of resources and opportunities, we can achieve more equality. Society, however, is not as simple as that. Many factors go into an individual's success. As an ally, be mindful of the ways you can address inequality through offering equitable solutions.

In the end, understanding intersectionalities, the importance of multiple voices, and the challenges of equity, will help us to create spaces so that everyone can succeed.

Creating Inclusive Spaces
Now that we have a basic understanding of intersectionality, equality and equity, we can use these ideas in a more practical manner to create safe spaces for members of the LGBTQIA+ community.

It is important to note here that many LGBTQIA+ individuals do not feel safe while being out in public. For example, when I am planning on going into a public space, I have to be very conscious about how I look and whether my physical appearance could make me the target of discrimination, especially if I have to use a public restroom. (I have experienced occasions when men have harassed me for using a women's restroom.) With this in mind, I make sure that I am presenting as more feminine so that I encounter less negativity if I have to use the restroom, as most public spaces do not offer an all-gender or family restroom. Unfortunately, this means that I often have to avoid using public restrooms in order to protect myself.

Many transgender individuals deal with such issues on a daily basis. You have the ability to help them by working to establish safe and inclusive spaces for all individuals. Bring this issue up with your place of employment, your school, and the businesses you patronize. Speak up against transphobic legislation that dictates that bathroom use should be determined by the sex a person is assigned at birth.

Medical Inclusion

Let's use the following example to examine the difficulties faced by LGBTQIA+ individuals in medical settings:

Sally, a transgender woman, has been seeing her primary care physician for some time, but experiences a sudden, acute medical condition that requires her to seek treatment in an emergency room. When she arrives and begins to fill out the medical forms, she sees that they require her to use her legally assigned name and sex. Sally has not legally changed her name, so she has to list her deadname, "Theodore," and list her sex as "male." She asks the staff person at the desk to please put her lived name, Sally, and her pronouns, she/her, on the forms.

When Sally is called for treatment, however, the nurse calls for "Theodore." Sally does not respond. The waiting room is full of people and she does not want them all to know that she is a transgender woman. The nurse calls for Therodore again, and this time the desk staff points at Sally, revealing her identity to the entire room.

Sally's problems continue when she is taken to the examination room, as her medical documents do not match her perceived identity. The doctor comes in expecting to be treating a man and is confused when seeing Sally. After Sally explains the situation, he rudely states, "Well, you have a penis, so why claim you're a woman?"

Despite her health emergency, Sally decides to leave the ER, as she is unsure whether she will receive the proper medical care due to the hospital's disregard for her identity. The institution and its staff have created a discriminatory space that has potentially affected the health outcomes of a patient.

Let's look at how these problems could be corrected.

Use Inclusive Language
Words have incredible power, and can be used to dehumanize or uplift. Do not assume to know how a person identifies. Medical spaces are one of the most difficult places for transgender individuals, with many opting to forego healthcare because they do not feel safe.

Provide Staff Training
It is crucial to provide training for all staff members, and to monitor them to ensure that they follow proper protocols. All training should be conducted by LGBTQIA+ individuals with medical backgrounds so that the staff learns about microaggressions and the ways that disrespecting sexual and gender identities harm patients.

Create A Welcoming Environment
All spaces accessed by medical staff and patients should include materials that are welcoming and inclusive. Reading materials and

walls posters is a good start. Have all staff members include their pronouns on name tags, which signals institutional awareness of the importance of identities. Additionally, designate restrooms and private spaces that are unisex, designed for one person, and available to anyone, regardless of gender. Some transgender individuals do not feel comfortable using a gendered restroom, and seek unisex spaces where they know they will be safe.

Listen to Feedback

Encourage patients to give feedback on their care. Do not just ask simple questions about how the staff performed, but also ask the patient if they felt safe and affirmed. Provide opportunities for patients to write about their experience. If negative feedback is submitted, do not dismiss it. Frequently, staff do not realize their actions or comments are perceived as hostile. Also, listen to feedback from staff members on how spaces can be improved and made safer and more welcoming.

Let's now look at the same example from before, using practices that create an inclusive and safe environment:

Sally, a transgender woman, has been seeing her primary care physician for some time, but experiences a sudden, acute medical condition that requires her to seek treatment in an emergency room. When she arrives and begins to fill out the medical forms, she sees that they require her to use her legally assigned name and sex. Sally has not legally changed her name, so she has to list her deadname, "Theodore," and list her sex as "male." She asks the staff person at the desk to please put her lived name, Sally, and her pronouns, she/her, on the forms. The desk nurse explains that she has inidcated this, and that each medical professional will only see her lived name and pronouns, as well as a note that she is a transgender woman.

When the nurse comes out, she sees that the name listed is "Sally," and calls for her. Sally responds and follows the nurse back to the exam room. When the doctor arrives, he introduces himself and states that his pronouns are he/him. He asks Sally to confirm her name, pronouns, and reason for needing treatment.

Sally feels much safer, knowing that the medical providers are treating her with the same respect and dignity that every patient deserves.

Sally stays and receives the care she needs.

As you can see, creating a safe and inclusive environment for LGBTQIA+ individuals does not mean treating them differently than any other person. LGBTQIA+ patients, especially transgender patients, don't want special treatment—they just seek respectful care from an affirming medical provider. Whether or not the medical staff "accepts" the patient's gender identity or sexuality is not relevant. Medical professionals are required by the federal Health Insurance Portability and Accountability Act (HIPAA) to serve patients to the highest possible standards. HIPAA protects patients' medical records and other personal health information. Doctors have also taken the Hippocratic Oath to do no harm to patients, including harm through actions and language. LGBTQIA+ individuals seeking medical attention are often extremely insecure about how they will be treated in medical settings. Showing them respect will help them feel more at ease, providing for better health care.

Academic Institutions

Today's youth are more aware of gender identities and sexuality than ever before. According to a 2020 study conducted by The Williams Institute, it is estimated that nearly two million youth between the ages of 13 and 17 identify as LGBTQ+ in the United States.[4] This number will only increase as more young people understand themselves in relation to their gender and sexuality.

There are many theories surrounding this increase, but I

believe it is largely due to visibility. When I first began to question my gender over two decades ago, there was little to no available information about gender identity. I either had to do extensive research on my home computer, or be lucky enough to know someone who wasn't cisgender. Today, gender diversity can be seen in all types of media. Being exposed to gender diversity at a young age does not encourage a child to become queer—rather, it normalizes a wide range of gender and sexual identities. Young people have the opportunity to openly question their gender and sexuality. They can determine how they best identify, rather than being forced to pretend to be someone they're not. The Drexel University School of Education says that, "[n]aturally, by exposing students to a diverse range of opinions, thoughts, and cultural backgrounds, you're encouraging them to be more open-minded later in life. This will make them open to new ideas and be able to attain a greater comprehension on a topic by taking in different points of view."[5]

This new-found understanding of gender identity, however, comes at a price. A *Washington Post* analysis of FBI data determined that

> School hate crimes targeting LGBTQ+ people have sharply risen in recent years, climbing fastest in states that have passed laws restricting LGBTQ+ student rights and education. ....The *Post* analysis found that the number of anti-LGBTQ+ school hate crimes serious enough to be reported to local police more than doubled nationwide between 2015-2019 (108 reported crimes) and 2021-2022 (232 reported crimes). The rise is steeper in the 28 states that have passed laws curbing the rights of trans-gender students at school and restricting how teachers can talk about issues of gender and sexuality.[6]

Creating an inclusive academic environment begins with the

understanding that everyone deserves to feel safe and respected. Establishing sexuality and gender-inclusive learning spaces does not promote a certain lifestyle, but encourages everyone to accept others' individual differences. For example, many school districts are currently facing challenges about whether they should display LGBTQ Pride flags in their buildings. Those who oppose the flags argue that they suggest that the schools approve of students becoming queer. I would argue that a teacher displaying a New York Yankees flag doesn't influence students to become fans of the team. Teachers display flags for different reasons, including making classrooms feel more comfortable, or to share something about themselves. Some say that if LGBTQ Pride flags are allowed, Confederate flags should also be displayed. The Confederate flag, however, historically represented an army that waged war against the United States, and in the present often signals discrimination and intolerance to many marginalized communities. Thus it has no place in a classroom.

Academic institutions displaying Pride flags show their support and acceptance for the LGBTQIA+ community. It is a simple way to say, "You are seen, you are accepted, and you are safe here." That message is needed now more than ever in our schools.

Here are some other ways that teachers can create an inclusive and safe classroom, even if they are not comfortable with the LGBTQIA+ community:

Use Inclusive Language
Just as in medical spaces, inclusive language is critical in creating a safe and inclusive classroom. Students should be asked to share their lived name and pronouns. Teachers and students should use those names and pronouns.

Students who come from other countries or ethnic groups should be called by their correct names—not shortened or

"Americanized" versions.

Some students' lived names and pronouns will change. Young people are in the process of discovering their identity. Respect and honor the changes.

If you wish, as a teacher, you can share your pronouns with students. If you are cisgender, this might seem unnecessary, but it is a simple action to show students that you are mindful of the many identities in their school.

Acknowledge Diverse Family Structures

LGBTQIA+ families are becoming more normalized, and many students might have parents or family members who identify as such. Teachers should therefore use inclusive language when speaking about parents/guardians, siblings, and extended families. Instead of saying "mom" or "dad" when referring to a student's parents, language such as "caregivers," "grownups," or "adults," is preferable.

Designate Gender Neutral Restrooms/Locker Rooms

Students should be able to use the restroom that aligns with their identity. Transphobic laws that force students to use restrooms that align with their sex at birth are extremely dangerous, and only lead to more harassment and mental anguish for students. In February 2023, a student named Nex Benedict was beaten in an Oklahoma public school restroom, and committed suicide shortly afterward.

Gender neutral or unisex restrooms and locker rooms provide LGBTQIA+ students with safe spaces. Eliminating gendered bathrooms and opting for single stall gender-neutral restrooms would be ideal. Often such restrooms already exist in a nurse's office, teacher's lounge, and in other places in a school building. Gender-neutral restrooms should be available to all students.

Create A Gay Straight Alliance (GSA) or LGBTQIA+ Community Club

A Gay Straight Alliance (GSA) or LGBTQIA+ club fosters a community in which LGBTQIA+ students and allies can come together in mutual support. GSAs also offer students the opportunity to learn about each other and spread positive messages to the entire school.

Do Not Tolerate Bullying

Being an LGBTQIA+ ally means standing up and advocating for all students. We know that bullying is extremely prevalent within our schools. Don't wait for someone else to address a bullying situation. It is never too late to create classroom expectations and rules against verbal, physical, and online bullying. This works best when students participate in setting the expectations. Involving students creates an environment in which everyone understands what behaviors are unacceptable, and the punishments when rules are broken.

Invest In Professional Development

It is important that professional development for teachers and staff is led by knowledgeable experts with experience in creating inclusive classrooms. I would recommend Transplaining as a resource for academic professional development.

Schools are a place of community for children and young adults. They can offer an environment that is safe and affirming, or one that is physically and emotionally harmful. All children, regardless of their age, deserve schools where they can express who they really are.

Remember that it is imperative to know the difference between creating equality and equity for students. "Equality" means providing all students equal support, while "equity" means providing appropriate support to students based on their needs. Don't be afraid to ask for help in creating a safe and inclusive space for students—the payoff can be life-saving. Inclusive classrooms are not just for LGBTQIA+ students, but for all students, including those who come from marginalized communities, and those with disabilities. Building equitable learning environments leads to greater achievement for all students.

Inclusion in the Home

LGBTQIA+ people are often rejected by their families due to their sexuality or gender identity. There are nearly 400,000 youth in the foster care system in the United States, with 30 percent identifying as LGBTQIA+.[7] According to the Human Rights Campaign, "LGBTQ+ youth enter the foster care system for many of the same reasons as non-LGBTQ+ youth in care, such as abuse, neglect, and parental substance abuse. Many LGBTQ+ youth have the added layer of trauma that comes with being rejected or mistreated because of their sexual orientation, gender identity or gender expression."[8]

These young people need a safe and inclusive place where they can express their sexuality or gender identity authentically. However, in late 2024, child welfare agencies in thirteen states "refuse[d] to place and provide services to children and families, including LGBTQ people and same-sex couples, if doing so conflict[ed] with their religious beliefs."[9] According to Youth. Gov, "78% of LGBTQIA+ youth in one study were removed or ran away from foster placements because of the caregiver's hostility toward their sexual orientation or gender identity."[10] Sixteen additional states do not have legal non-discrimination policies to permit protect LGBTQIA+ parents rights to foster or adopt children.

Hostility towards LGBTQIA+ youth is very prevalent in the foster care system, resulting in the dire need for nationwide non-discrimination policies that allow LGBTQIA+ adults the opportunity to foster or adopt these children. Just like any child,

LGBTQIA+ youth need an affirming home where they can live in safety.

That is why choosing to transform your home into a loving, affirming, and welcoming space is a must when becoming an ally. Whether LGBTQIA+ people are part of your family, or guests who might visit you for a short time, you want everyone to feel comfortable and safe. You also want to foster a place of learning, where your family is open to questioning and discovering new ideas and ways of life.

As an ally, there are things you can do to create an inclusive and safe space in your home. Simple actions, such as displaying Pride flags or affirming yard signs are an important first step. Consider these other suggestions:

Welcome All
In creating a welcoming home, be intentional and mindful about how you decorate gathering spaces. For example, some LGBTQIA+ individuals have experienced rejection in religious communities, and might find a space unwelcoming if your home contains numerous symbols of faith. You don't need to remove these items completely, but think about placing them in private areas.

Allow Questions
Whether you have an LGBTQIA+ family member or not, establish an environment where children feel safe to ask questions, even if you don't know the answers. Growing up, I did not feel safe to ask questions about sexuality or gender because these so-called "abnormal" identities were either mocked, criticized, or completely ignored.

The more open you are, the more inclusionary and welcoming your home will become. It is normal for children to be curious about different ways of life, so help them seek answers through web searches, media from reputable sources, age-appropriate books, and conversations. The key is to make sure you use reliable resources, created by those who are living authentically. Don't be afraid to answer questions by saying, "I don't know, but let's find out."

Be an Active Listener and Learner

When you are engaging with a different race, culture, identity, or religion from your own, do so with an open mind. Active listening and learning means engaging with a person through respectful conversation. Ask questions without being rude or inappropriate. For example, never ask a transgender person what genitalia they possess! That type of question is never acceptable, no matter how "open" you are trying to be.

Workplace Inclusion

Many people believe that the office is just a place where we go to earn a paycheck. The reality is that we spend years of our lives at work. Which is why creating a safe and inclusive workplace, where everyone feels comfortable, is so important.

Unfortunately, the office is often the hardest place for LGBTQIA+ individuals to feel affirmed and accepted. A 2022 survey conducted by the Center for American Progress found that "[h]alf of LGBTQI+ adults reported experiencing some form of workplace discrimination or harassment in the past year because of their sexual orientation, gender identity, or intersex status, including being fired; being denied a promotion; having their work hours cut; or experiencing verbal, physical, or sexual harassment."[11]

Consider these steps in implementing an affirming workplace culture:

Pronoun Inclusive Markers

- Include the pronouns of each person, not just LGBTQ-IA+ people, on name tags and in email signatures.

- Include pronouns in all data collection forms, for both

clients and workers.

- When collecting data, have a place for people to place their chosen/lived names. Legal names must sometimes be documented, but chosen names can always be added in a space that asks the person's preferred name.

Gender Inclusive Dress Codes

Workplaces have historically supported the belief that all individuals should fit neatly into the gender binary and identify as either "male" or "female." They might even have had a dress code in which employees had to wear articles of clothing based on their specific work responsibilities and gender. Eliminating a gender-based dress code is a major step toward erasing gender-identity discrimination.

In 2022, Virgin Airlines updated its dress code to allow the free expression of its employees' gender identity in their work uniforms. Writing in *The Independent*, Lucy Thackray reported that, "[t]he change means that male employees may wear skirt suits to work, if they so wish, while women and gender-non-conforming staff may opt for trouser suits without being asked to wear the traditional female uniform. It followed a previous relaxation on rules regarding visible tattoos and piercings in May 2022. The airline also created optional pronoun badges for either staff or customers to wear, in a bid to avoid people being misgendered on board its planes."[12]

Allowing people to express their identity in their work attire is truly inclusive. Virgin Airlines did not compromise its professional uniform for employees, but rather allowed each employee to showcase their individuality, regardless of gender or identity. A person does not need to be feminine in order to wear a skirt, nor does a person need to be masculine to wear a suit.

Build Community

As in schools, creating an organizational Gay Straight Alliance fosters a sense of community between LGBTQIA+ employees and their allies. These types of groups can assist with improving the work climate, discussing problems, and ensuring a safe space for LGBTQIA+ staff members.

A greater understanding of the work environment may be gained through short questionnaires. Taking time in meetings to assist staff with getting to know each other will also positively contribute to the workplace climate.

Keep in mind that an individual's gender identity and sexuality are private. Never force anyone to "out" themselves at work. I think of the episode of *The Office* where Michael Scott learns that Oscar is gay. Michael starts behaving differently towards Oscar, eventually forcing him to reveal his sexuality to the entire staff before he was ready to do so. Allow people to come out in their own time and in their own way—and remember to respect their confidentiality!

Be Visible
Be proud of creating an inclusive workplace! Demonstrate your inclusiveness and acceptance through everyday actions.

Hire an Inclusion Officer to support best practices that ensure the safety of all employees.

Create an inclusion policy and stick to it! Everyone needs to see, read, and understand the policy and it must be something that all are expected to adhere to.

Provide Professional Development
Invest in professional development conducted by educators who are knowledgeable about inclusion practices, and experienced in their implementation.

Do not ask or expect employees or coworkers who identify with the LGBTQIA+ community to educate others. That is the job of trained professionals.

Do not allow non-inclusive acts against your LGBTQIA+ or other marginalized employees to go unchecked. However, do not assume that the perpetrator acted maliciously. An article in Superscript on creating inclusive workplaces suggests that

> Calling [the perpetrator] out assumes the worst and assumes that the motivation for someone's hurtful comments or actions are malicious, when they could just as easily be the result of momentary thoughtlessness, ignorance or naivety. Calling in [which means that we should address situations in a private manner with a focus on educating rather than punishment] assumes that we're all human, we make mistakes and we want to learn how to do better. It encourages changes in behavior rather than demonizing mistakes.[13]

Use Non-Gendered and Inclusive Language
Inclusive language is something that most of us need to improve on, as gendered language is so ingrained into our speech. In the workplace, focus on using speech that is non-gendered and inclusive of multiple identities.

- Instead of using "ladies and gentlemen," use "esteemed colleagues."
- Educate yourself on gender-neutral titles such as the following:
  - Mx. pronounced "mix"
  - Mre. pronounced "mystery"
  - Pr. pronounced "per" and short for person
  - Mir. pronounced "mer"
  - Msr. pronounced "misser"

- Nb. pronounced "en-bee"
- Ser. pronounced "sair"
- Zr. pronounced "zeester"
- Tiz. pronounced "tizz" short for citizen
- Mv. a proposed title specifically for addressing a maverique person.

Here is a table to help you see what inclusive terms should be introduced into the workplace:

Non Inclusive Terms	Inclusive Terms
Hi guys, ladies, gentlemen	Hi all, folks, team, friends, team, everybody, everyone, y'all, or specific terms like customers, clients, employees, boyfriend, girlfriend, husband, wife, partners, spouse
Best man for the job	Best person for the job
That man, woman	That person
Sexual preference	Sexual orientation, sexuality
A person's sex	A person's gender identity
Decided to be/become a man or woman	They transitioned their gender identity
Each employee should read his handbook	Employees should read the handbook

Establishing an affirming workplace culture requires buy-in from everyone. Educate the people at your workplace to why these steps are being implemented and how it will benefit them, even if your workplace does not currently employ a self-identified LGBTQIA+ individual. Chances are very good that someone in your workplace is closeted, and does not feel safe to come out.

A safe and affirming workplace also increases productivity.

"Inclusive workplaces ensure employees are safe, respected and able to fully contribute," says Jackie Ferguson of The Diversity Movement. "An Oxford study showed that employees that are happy at work are 13% more productive, which means greater profitability for any business."[14] Inclusive business practices benefit workers—and the bottom line.

The Reward Will Far Exceed the Effort

Creating inclusive spaces can be difficult. You will face challenges. People are resistant to change, but change is needed. According to Lacie Blankenship of Vanderbilt University's Owen Graduate School of Management,

> Inclusion isn't something that can happen overnight; it takes time. There is vast room for improvement regarding LGBTQIA+ inclusivity in the business world. A key aspect of becoming more inclusive is to stay open-minded, listen to others, and welcome feedback. True leaders will proactively look for ways to include everyone and take action when new perspectives are presented.[15]

It will take time, patience, and effort to create truly inclusive spaces, but in the end, the reward will far exceed the effort.

Summary: Intersectionality and Creating Safe Spaces

- What is Intersectionality?
- Equity vs. Equality
- Creating Inclusive Spaces
- Medical Inclusion
  - *Use Inclusive Language*
  - *Provide Staff Training*
  - *Create a Welcoming Environment*
  - *Listen to Feedback*
- Academic Inclusion
  - *Use Inclusive Language*
  - *Acknowledge Diverse Family Structures*
  - *Designate Gender Neutral Restrooms/Locker Rooms*
  - *Create a Gay Straight Alliance (GSA) or LGBTQ+ Community Club*
  - *Do Not Tolerate Bullying*
  - *Invest in Professional Development*
- Inclusion in the Home
  - *Welcome All*
  - *Allow Questions*
  - *Be an Active Listener and Learner*

- Workplace Inclusion
  - *Pronoun Inclusive Markers*
  - *Gender Inclusive Dress Codes*
  - *Build Community*
  - *Be Visible*
  - *Provide Professional Development*
  - *Use Non-Gendered and Inclusive Language*

10. Being An Ally to Someone Who Is Coming Out

I did not come out; rather I allowed you to come into my life.

Coming out is one of the most difficult things for an LGBTQIA+ individual to do. The process is extremely stressful, as the person never knows how others—family members, friends, coworkers, even strangers—will react. We have all heard horror stories associated with coming out—LGBTQIA+ people who are kicked out of families, lose their housing, their jobs, friends, and more. These stories plague closeted people, leaving them in terror about what might happen to them. It is particularly bad in the current environment, as there were 356 reported acts of violence towards an LGBTQIA+ person or the larger community between June 2022 and April 2023 in the United States.[1] That is almost one incident per day! Given the dangers of living "out" in our nation, coming out is an act of extreme courage.

Many people put so much importance on coming out that any negative response can be devastating. Therefore, as an ally it is crucial to be respectful and affirming. If someone comes out to you, understand that it's an amazing gift, as it means the person trusts you enough to share who they truly are. Be gracious, as it is an important, joyous moment. Respect the person. Be patient. Don't make a comment such as, "Yeah, I always knew you were _____." Instead, listen and allow the person to share their identity with you. Accept whatever they say, and don't tell them who you think they are. They are coming out because they want to be comfortable with you on their terms, not yours.

As I have mentioned previously, be sure to respect the person's confidentiality. Their identity is theirs alone, and not to be shared with others. Just because they came out to you does not mean that you can discuss their identity with anyone else. When a person is coming out, they are very selective in who they confide in. They may not feel safe enough with other people in their lives to come out to them yet. No person comes out to everyone at once! The process takes a lot of time, as the person decides who they can trust.

Now that your LGBTQIA+ person has come out to you, offer them unconditional love. Accept them for who they are, with no strings attached. When a person comes out, you are not losing them, but are actually gaining a deeper and more honest relationship. Tell them that you care about them and love them for who they are. And, it is okay to go through a grieving period for the person you once knew.

Those All-Important Questions

It is only natural to have questions for a person when they come out. Please ask permission before beginning an "interrogation" about their choices. Do not assume you can just ask them anything and everything. If they allow you to ask questions, make sure they are appropriate. Don't ask anything that places some form of blame on the person coming out.

Most people expect to answer questions after they come out. Understand that they may not have all the answers to your questions, as they still might be discovering themselves and their identity. Be respectful with your questions, and remember that they are still the same person that they were before coming out. Do not make assumptions that you know what the person needs. Ask them if there is anything you can do for them. Offer your support and assure them that you are there for them. Once again, they may not know what they need from you, and that is okay! Just being there for them with love and support is a great way to start.

Avoid saying the following things when someone comes out to you:

167

"My new _____ friend."

Their identity does not change their relationship with you. They are the same person they were before coming out.

"Why did you wait so long?"

Everyone comes out on their own timetable. Not everyone has known that they were LGBTQIA+ their entire lives. That doesn't make their coming out any less valid.

"When did you decide to be _____?"

Being LGBTQIA+ is not a choice or a decision that someone makes—it is a part of who they are. The choice is choosing to overcome the fear and come out.

"But my religion says being _____ is a sin."

Your religious beliefs should not influence the lives of others and do not give you the right to decide how they should express themselves. If your religion does not accept LGBTQIA+ identities, you should nonetheless love and respect the people who live them. Practice loving others for who they are, regardless of your beliefs.

"You're not into me, are you?"

If a heterosexual friend does not have a crush on every member of the opposite sex, then neither does your LGBTQIA+ friend.

"Are you the top or bottom?"

A person's sexual engagements are not open for discussion. There is no need to ask someone what their preferences are in the bedroom.

"What happened to you? You changed."

Your LGBTQIA+ person did not change into someone else. If there is a change, it is for the better, as they are expressing their true selves now and trusting you with that.

Lastly, be there for your LGBTQIA+ person! Coming out is a very difficult process, and that person has probably lost some friends or family members along the way. This can be very isolating and can result in mental health challenges. Be present and supportive for them. Help them find organizations that offer community and support.

Loving An LGBTQIA+ Individual

Coming out doesn't just affect the person who actually comes out—it affects everyone in their life. Yes, the person coming out has given a lot of thought to how their coming out will affect the people around them. It is normal to experience a grieving period after someone has come out to you, especially if that person is a family member. It can be a shock to learn that your child, partner, friend, loved one, etc., has come out as LGBTQIA+. Everyone goes through the conventional stages of grieving, but there is not a timetable to how long this period will take. For some people, it is quick. For others, it can last years. I cannot think of a better person to explain this than my wife, Katie.

Katie's Story

NV tells me that there are many spouses and loved ones of transgender individuals that would benefit from hearing my perspective on our queer marriage. While it touches my heart to hear that so many people look at our relationship for hope and inspiration, our marriage is nothing extraordinary. We have a successful marriage for the same reasons that make any marriage successful—we both invest in our relationship and communicate with each other.

NV and I were close friends before we started dating and now they are hands down my best friend. Anything I'm interested in doing I want to do with them. I talk to them about everything, they know practically everything about me. Isn't that how it should be? Shouldn't the person that you're married to be your best friend? This is why it puzzles me that people are so interested in our relationship.

Yes, I am a straight woman who is in love with and married to a trans femme genderfluid person, but our marriage is not defined by how we view our respective genders or sexual preferences. Who NV is on the inside is what matters and that has not changed since they came out. If anything, it shines more brightly because they came out: that happy, nerdy, passionate, kind person I fell in love with in high school.

Has it been easy? No. When NV came out I went through a grieving process, not because the person I am married to was not who I thought they were, but because my vision for our future had to be adjusted—and that's okay. My grief was directed at how I would be able to express our love and relationship to the world around me. I knew that their coming out was going to change everything, as so many people struggle to understand why a person transitions genders.

Now I have to defend and explain who NV is and their gender identity, while also defending my own sexuality. Coming out was not just about their gender identity, but also about my allyship to them and the entire community. Coming out affects the lives of everyone, not just the person coming out, and grief is a normal part of becoming an ally to them.

Any marriage can be rocked by a career change, financial struggles, medical needs, or fertility issues. The important thing is to communicate with your partner, which is something NV and I are pretty good at. Therapy is also a great thing. I saw a therapist during my grieving process, which helped immensely. So too is having a support network of friends and chosen family.

If anyone is experiencing a change in their relationship due to a partner coming out, I would like to offer this advice based on my experiences. Number one, communicate your thoughts and feelings because they deserve just as much consideration as your partner's. Number two, it's okay to grieve. Number three, find support where it makes sense for you, whether that is a therapist, a close friend, a family member or a group like Pflag, Stand with Trans, the Trevor Project, or Advocates for Trans Equality. You can also check your local LGBTQ Center for support groups.

Finally to all the queer humans out there that want the type of relationship that we have, don't give up, your person is out there and they will love you exactly as you are. Everyone's path is unique. Allow yourself to feel your emotions and express your thoughts with your loved ones.

Our experiences are our own, and not everyone will navigate the coming out process and grieving period as Katie and I did. One of the best ways to help you during your grieving period is to seek out advice and support from others who have gone through it. And as Katie said, I highly suggest reaching out to the LGBTQ community centers in your area, or to organizations such as PFLAG, Human Rights Campaign, Advocates for Trans Equality, Parents of Trans Youth, Strong Family Alliance,

Rainbow Families, The Trevor Project, Gender Spectrum, or Straight for Equality. Organizations like these provide support for all members of the LGBTQIA+ community and their allies.

Remember one thing—you are not losing that person. If anything, your relationship will only grow and become stronger.

Coming Out Is A Lifetime Journey

Many LGBTQIA+ individuals feel like they have to wait until the "perfect" time to come out, or that they are "too old" to come out. However, coming out does not have a recommended age. We all discover ourselves on our own time, and come out when it is best for us. Whether a person is eight or eighty, they deserve to express themselves as they understand their gender or sexuality.

A person might first come out as gay, and then discover later on that they are nonbinary. Sometimes a person might come out as a cross-dresser, and then discover that they are transgender. Like any person, LGBTQIA+ individuals discover new aspects of their identity as they age. This does not invalidate their earlier feelings. Most people change their clothing and hairstyles over the course of their lives, matching their outward appearance with their sense of themselves. This is normal and valid, just as growing in your understanding of gender identity or sexual orientation is normal and valid.

Whatever the sexual orientation or gender identity of your friend, coworker, loved one, or classmate, everyone deserves to be treated with love and support. If you employ the advice offered above, you will excel in your role as an ally. Remember that we all want to live our lives as we see ourselves. Being an LGBTQIA+ person is beautiful. Who they love or how they identify their gender and sexuality does not change who they are.

Your feelings are valid, too, and we all deserve the time to understand and accept the changes in our lives. Remember that you are not alone. It's okay to lean on others for support. You don't need to handle this on your own.

Summary: Being An Ally to Someone Who is Coming Out

- Those All Important Questions
- Loving an LGBTQIA+ Individual
- Katie's Story
- Coming Out Is A lifetime Journey

11. Religion and the LGBTQIA+ Community

No matter what, use your faith as a tool to promote love, acceptance, inclusion, and equity for all mankind; not just those who are similar to you.

One of the main sources of trauma for LGBTQIA+ individuals is religion. While there are religious communities that affirm LGBTQIA+ rights, many preach a narrative of rejection and hate, claiming their faith does not sanction any lifestyle that does not fit into the heterosexual norm. Some religious sects have even called for open abuse and imprisonment of LGBTQIA+ individuals. These messages are not only discriminatory, but lead to emotional anguish and personal trauma for many in the LGBTQIA+ community.

This chapter will examine the need for all religions to return to their true guiding principles of love and acceptance in order to support the LGBTQIA+ community.. I do not expect everyone to agree with me on this; however, I do hope you can keep an open mind and ask yourself how you can use your own faith to be an affirming LGBTQIA+ ally.

Facing My Own Faith

Religion is a very important part of my intersectional identity. I was raised in a Christian household and taught the beliefs of our family church. There, I learned that I had to be "good enough" to gain entry into heaven upon my death, rather than spending eternity in the torments of hell. I was also told that being queer was evil, making it difficult for me to find faith and comfort in the church. I distinctly remember one Sunday when the pastor called for any person who might have "queer" thoughts or inclinations to come forward so he could "pray the gay away from them." Needless to say, I sat quietly, hoping that he wouldn't look in my direction and single me out.

Because of my religious upbringing,, when I came out, I felt that I had to leave my faith behind, believing that I could no longer be a Christian because God had rejected me. It took a long time for me to unlearn the traumatic religious lessons of my youth. Eventually, I was able to find an affirming church with a pastor who preached love and inclusion for all people, regardless of their gender or sexuality. It was through this church and its congregation that I was able to find my faith again and understand that at its heart, Christianity seeks to teach us that God loves us all, no matter who we are. Most religions have similar messages, yet many have been twisted and distorted to exclude those who don't fit in with their narrow ideology. Unfortunately, those who preach hatred towards the LGBTQIA+ community often have the loudest voices and cause the most damage.

Since coming out, I have learned that at its core, religion should represent love and compassion for all. Working with affirming religious leaders has helped me understand that we are not meant to impose our beliefs on others, but rather to use those beliefs to help improve the world around us. We are not meant to fight a war against evil. Instead, we are meant to create a world of welcoming acceptance and empathy. This advice and wisdom can assist on your path towards becoming an affirming and inclusive ally.

Being that I adhere to Christianity, I have focused this chapter on that religion; however, the lessons can be applied to other forms of religion and spirituality. I recommended that after reading this, you begin to question how your faith portrays the LGBTQIA+ community.

I learned a great deal while composing this chapter, and discovered that my religious imperative honors the biblical

THE QUEER ALLIES BIBLE

golden rule: "Therefore all things whatsoever ye would that men should do to you, do ye even so to them: for this is the law and the prophets." (Mt. 7:12 KJV).

What is the problem?

According to the non-profit organization LOVEboldly:

> The Christian church has earned a reputation for being anti-LGBTQIA+. In some cases, the church has been openly hostile to LGBTQIA+ people, treating them like outcasts rather than siblings and children of God. In other cases, the church has remained silent rather than follow the example of Jesus. As a result, LGBTQIA+, straight, and cisgender Christians have left the church or have given up on their faith because they feel unsafe, unable to engage sincere questions, and unwelcome from communities where they can authentically grow in their faith.[1]

For many in the church, the true message of Jesus—as one who preached for the inclusion of all, not just a select few—has been lost. As Reverend Amy Aspey, the lead pastor at Short North United Methodist Church in Columbus, Ohio puts it, "The gospel is about transformation, and transformation means that it is going to cost you something. Christianity is a radical religion with its message being one of liberation from oppression, not exclusion."[2] Reverend Aspey's church practices an inclusive and affirming message towards the LGBTQIA+ and all marginalized communities.

New Testament Christianity is built upon our understanding of the teachings of Jesus Christ, who charges us with the task of supporting and welcoming all people, regardless of their identities or beliefs. Jesus surrounded himself with those deemed unworthy by the powerful, such as the impoverished, sex workers, foreigners, and the disabled. Far too many contemporary churches and leaders preach Chrisitianity while rejecting anyone who doesn't follow their strict ideals and narrow imaginings of identity politics.

Before we approach certain biblical passages, it is important to point out that every translation of the Christian Bible approaches the doctrine differently, and may contain some variation within scripture, psalms, and passages. According to history.com, "more than four centuries after its publication, the King James Bible (a.k.a. the King James Version, or simply the Authorized Version) remains the most famous Bible translation in history—and one of the most printed books ever."[3] Does that mean that the King James Version is the most reliable or accurate version of the Bible? That question is hard to answer, as the Bible was not originally written in English. Each version varies due to the complexities of translating ancient Greek, Hebrew, or Aramaic into our modern languages. According to Abraham Smith, Professor of New Testament at the Perkins School of Theology at Southern Methodist University, "[t]he New Revised Standard Version Updated Edition (NRSVue) has become the most historically accurate, compellingly clear, and broadly vetted English translation in the world. Academic reliability and everyday readability meet each other on every page."[4] Nonetheless, due to its popularity and use among English readers, I will use the King James Version when quoting from scripture.

Often, those who oppose inclusion of the LGBTQIA+ community within Christianity cite certain Bible passages to justify their actions. For example, Leviticus 18:22 is often interpreted as condemning homosexuality: "Thou shalt not lie with mankind, as with womankind: it is abomination." (Lev 18:22 KJV.) While the passage is often wielded for political means, biblical scholars offer differing interpretations of what it really means. According to Queer Bible Hermeneutics, a blog dedicated to examining the Bible through LGBTQIA+ perspectives:

Most traditional English translations interpret Leviticus 18:22 as a divine condemnation of erotic, same-sex relationships. However, careful philological, literary analysis of the original Hebrew shows another interpretation: a divine condemnation of same-sex rape. The original Hebrew is more ambiguous than the traditional English translation. Instead of practicing the principle of lectio difficilior probabilitor, "the more difficult reading and more likely reading," modern translators dispel ambiguity by making the translation as simple as possible.[5]

It's not just Leviticus 18:22; a majority of scripture used by the Christian church against LGBTQIA+ people is contradicted by its ancient Hebrew and Greek interpretations. This includes Corinthians 1:

Know ye not that the unrighteous shall not inherit the kingdom of God? Be not deceived: neither fornicators, nor idolaters, nor adulterers, nor effeminate, nor abusers of themselves with mankind, Nor thieves, nor covetous, nor drunkards, nor revilers, nor extortioners, shall inherit the kingdom of God. And such were some of you: but ye are washed, but ye are sanctified, but ye are justified in the name of the Lord Jesus, and by the Spirit of our God (1 Cor. 6:9-11 KJV).

And Timothy 1:

For whoremongers, for them that defile themselves with mankind, for menstealers, for liars, for perjured persons, and if there be any other thing that is contrary to sound doctrine; According to the glorious gospel of the blessed God, which was committed to my trust (1 Tim. 1:10-11 KJV).

The mistranslation of the ancient Greek words "malakoi" and "arsenokoitai" has led to a deeply damaging use of these texts. Matthew Vines of The Reformation Project, an LGBTQIA+ affirming Christian organization, offers an alternate version of these passages:

> Timothy 1:10-11… uses the term "arsenokoitai" in a… "vice list." Given that many Bible translations since 1946 have rendered "malakoi" and "arsenokoitai "as "homosexuals" or "men who have sex with men," it's worth taking a close look at these two Greek terms. The term malakoi literally means "soft," and it was widely used to describe a lack of self-control, weakness, cowardice, and laziness. Although most uses of the term in ancient literature were not related to sexual behavior, men who took the passive role in same-sex relations were sometimes called malakoi, which is why many non-affirming Christians argue that it represents a condemnation of same-sex relationships. But even in sexual contexts, "malakoi" was most frequently used to describe men who were seen as lacking self-control in their love for women. It's only in the past century that many Bible translators have connected the word specifically to same-sex relationships. More common English translations in past centuries were terms such as "weaklings," "wantons," and "debauchers."[6]

The Bible is filled with stories meant to teach us how to behave toward one another. Updating it through translation was a means of aligning the text to the beliefs of particular communities. The 2022 documentary film *1946: The Mistranslation That Shifted*

Culture, argues that the Revised Standard Version (RSV) translation of the Bible, published in 1952, led to the Christian anti-gay movement. Examining never-before-seen archives at Yale University, the film discusses how mistranslation has engendered anti-LGBTQIA+ hostility and discrimination. Reverend David S. Fearon provides a powerful statement in the film regarding the inclusion of the word homosexual in 1 Corinthians 6: 9-10: "I am more deeply concerned because well-meaning and sincere, but misinformed and misguided people may use this Revised Standard Version translation of I Corinthians 6:9-10 as a sacred weapon."[7]

The Book of Romans, written by Paul in 57 CE, contains what is thought to be the first reference to homosexuality in the New Testament:

> For this cause God gave them up unto vile affections: for even their women did change the natural use into that which is against nature: And likewise also the men, leaving the natural use of the woman, burned in their lust one toward another; men with men working that which is unseemly, and receiving in themselves that recompence of their error which was meet (Rom. 1:26-27 KJV).

However, the passage is not a direct teaching of Jesus, as Paul was not one of the twelve disciples and never knew Jesus. According to Reverend Aspey,

> Saul was a zealous and enthusiastic persecutor of the early church. Saul was highly educated and passionate about the traditions of his Jewish ancestors. His spiritual life was rigorous and steeped in study, fasting and prayer. Saul the persecutor becomes Paul the missionary.

Perhaps, he goes by a new name to symbolize this change to both himself and the world.[8]

The society and culture of Paul's time shaped his understandings and beliefs, which is exactly why interpreting his words as "law" today is a mistake. Reverend Aspey adds that,

Hair length and head coverings have generally become understood as cultural customs and ancient notions of gender roles. But, when it comes to sex-same relationships today, it somehow becomes a universal truth. Even when loving same-sex relationships is not at all what is referenced in the ancient context. When we superimpose the ancient context onto our context, we make a mess because the ancient crashes with the present in ways that do not build up the body of Christ.[9]

In addition, Psalm 139 is often used as a justification for the rejection of transgender people: "For thou hast possessed my reins: thou hast covered me in my mother's womb. I will praise thee; for I am fearfully and wonderfully made: marvelous are thy works; and that my soul knoweth right well." (Ps. 139:13-14 KJV). Similarly, transgender and nonbinary identities are often rejected because of Genesis 1:27: "So God created man in his own image, in the image of God created he him; male and female created he them." (Gen. 1:27 KJV)

Despite this seemingly blunt language, we must remember that translation, shifting attitudes about gender presentation, and cultural change has had an untold impact on how we choose to interpret the Bible. Scholars and activists alike have used the Bible as an opportunity to reexamine Christian figures, As evidenced by recent theological debate, some claim that according to the Old Testament and the Talmud, Adam can be identified as androgynous, thus, complicating our previously binary understanding of Adam and Eve:

> In the Babylonian Talmud, documents compiled over the 3rd to 5th centuries, ancient Jewish scholars acknowledged this verse was not a denial of a person being both. They believe Genesis indicated that not only was humanity at large "male and female" but the first human (Adam) was too. They believed Adam had two sides, a male side and a female side that existed together in harmony. To further support this interpretation, it isn't until this earthling is put to sleep that male and female emerge and we start to get different Hebrew words for them: "ish" and "ishah." In Genesis 2:22, we get the story of God taking one of Adam's ribs to create Eve. This is a mistranslation since the Hebrew word for "rib" that is used in this verse does not mean "rib" but rather means "side". Extra-biblical Hebrew texts also never use that word to mean "rib" because there is a dedicated word for "rib" that is used in other places in Genesis. If we reread this verse with the word "rib" translated as "side", we can interpret that Adam or the earthling is split into two, the male side and the female side. This interpretation not only supports that Adam is genderqueer but also supports a feminist interpretation that males and females were created equally.[10]

This interpretation is rooted in a critical reading of the Earth's creation that emphasizes the existence of the non-binary elements of everyday life, such as dawn and twilight and most urgently, genderqueer existence.

While these passages are used to exclude and discriminate against the LGBTQIA+ community, there are many more Bible verses that teach inclusivity and condemn petty judgements, such as Galatians 3:28: "There is neither Jew nor Greek, there is neither bond nor free, there is neither male nor female: for ye are all one in Christ Jesus."

And Ephesians 2:14-16:

For he is our peace, who hath made both one, and hath broken down the middle wall of partition between us; Having abolished in his flesh the enmity, even the law of commandments contained in ordinances; for to make in himself of twain one new man, so making peace; And that he might reconcile both unto God in one body by the cross, having slain the enmity thereby.

We must ask ourselves: why are the verses that encourage humility and acceptance ignored by many congregations in favor of those that can be interpreted as a judgment of others? The former serve as a reminder that we all are equal and valid in the eyes of Christ, rather than elevating some as superior to others. Galatians 3:28: and Ephesians 2:14-16 encourage Christians to view everyone as equals, and to respect the teaching that all humans are the same under the eyes of God. Reverend Aspey states that,

As followers of Jesus, in wrestling with any text, it's crucial to see what Jesus has to say about it. Jesus says nothing about same-sex relationships, and Rabbi Jesus, who was Jewish, knew the Torah, too. Jesus taught about love and also showed us what this looks like. Building the Kingdom of God is one that centers those on the margins. He literally celebrated an open table and hung out with prostitutes and tax collectors and women and lepers. The religious leaders of the day kept telling people they didn't belong, and Jesus kept showing them, over and over again, that this is just not true.[11]

There is a great deal of evidence that being exclusionary does not fit with Christian fellowship. Reverend Aspey says that "[p]erhaps the lesson here is realizing how dangerous it is to take a piece of Scripture and turn it into Gospel truth when it doesn't align with the Gospel of Jesus."[12] Applying some aspects of the scripture as "divine truth" and neglecting others mirror the hypocrisy that led Jesus to rebel against the religious leaders of his day. Reverend Aspey offers these words for Chrisitians who seek to become allies to the LGBTQIA+ community:

Challenge yourself in how you use your voice for inclusion, which will look different for everyone. People will find themselves in different social circles, whether physical or virtual, which can determine how effective they feel their voice may be. Understanding and creating intentional inclusionary speech with your conversations and your actions is key, along with how you spend your money. There is nothing about spiritual growth that is comfortable. If you do find yourself in a deep place of comfort, I would ask if it isn't because of a degree of complacency, and if so what that might mean. The good news of Jesus that it actually does say throughout scripture is good news for all people. His life, his death, and his resurrection were good news for all people. So we don't get to take the all out of all people. The gospel is about transformation. Transformation means that it's going to cost you something; change is going to cost you something.[13]

While homosexuality and gender diversity have seen mixed interpretations and understandings throughout history, it is important to keep in mind that these liberation movements will continue to strengthen and grow as our society evolves.

Therefore, focusing not on the literal interpretations of the text, but rather their meanings and lessons, is key. Historical spiritual texts must be understood through the context of our modern needs, not interpreted to govern our modern lives from outdated or discriminatory perspectives. Rabbi Ari Jun, Director of Cincinnati's Jewish Community Relations Council, offers the following advice for anyone seeking to become an affirming and inclusive ally to the LGBTQIA+ community while still holding true to their faith and traditions:

> I believe we would do a lot better when we interact with and get to know people as individuals rather than trying to understand them through larger structures. I have seen such animosity with regard to drag performances and drag storytimes from Jews, and it almost never involves people who have real relationships with those who are affected and those who are in the community the people who are directing their hatred at. They've never talked to such folks. They have no idea why it's happening. They're just very angry about it. When you can have that kind of personal interaction with those who you are directing hatred towards, it is so much harder to disregard the person right in front of you and imagine that they must be evil when they look just like your son or your daughter. We do a very poor job within society at humanizing each other, and almost to the contrary we love finding others in our society. Gender identity and sexual orientation are two spaces where it's very easy to find visceral topics, as they're very closely tied to how we see ourselves within the world. Getting to know folks and humanizing them, I think it's a big step towards healing us all.[14]

As Rabbi Jun points out, it becomes a lot more difficult to

spread hatred against a group of people when you have had open conversations with them and gotten to know them better. We do not have to agree with everyone, but we must understand that our world is made up of over seven billion people who all have a unique individuality to them.

Honoring one's faith is not about trying to use spiritual texts to justify prejudices and discrimination, but rather learning how to respect each other for what makes humans so resilient: unity in diversity. The very concept of finding strength in our differences can be credited to Sufi philosopher Ibn al-'Arabi and is referred to as wahdat al-wujud ("unity of being.")[15]

Use your faith to create the kingdom of heaven here on earth. Build it through compassion, acceptance, respect, affirmations, and love. Converse with members of marginalized groups. See God's beauty in their lives. Support churches that welcome the LGBTQIA+ community and seek to be inclusive and affirming to all. Remember that faith built upon condemnation of others is as stable as a house built on a foundation of sand.

Rethinking Our Faith

This chapter was particularly important for me to write, as one of the greatest forms of LGBTQIA+ hate and discrimination comes from religious messaging. Whether from organized churches like Westboro Baptist Church, or from political and government leaders justifying their discriminatory policies, religion has frequently been tainted in order to influence a cisnormative heteronormative culture and society. While all religions have different practices and beliefs, at their core, they believe in love and acceptance. Using religion and spiritual texts to justify discrimination of any marginalized community or individual is blasphemy.

This is nothing new unfortunately, as religion has been used as a tool of hate for centuries. For example, slave owners during the transatlantic slave trade referred to their captives as "sons of

Ham," likening enslaved Africans to Ham, who was "blackened" by the sin of gazing upon his naked father. (Genesis 9:18–27 KJV). Similarly, Apostle Paul's Epistle to the Ephesians 6:5-7 was also exploited by pro-slavery advocates:[16]

> Servants, be obedient to them that are your masters according to the flesh, with fear and trembling, in singleness of your heart, as unto Christ; Not with eyeservice, as menpleasers; but as the servants of Christ, doing the will of God from the heart; With good will doing service, as to the Lord, and not to men.

We all recognize that slavery is not what The Creator, or whomever you believe in, intended for anyone, yet spiritual texts were used to justify it. However, Paul's message was not a justification of slavery, but a call for patience and love, no matter how difficult your situation. We will never live in a world that is truly accepting and affirming; yet we have to continue to trust in the message of acceptance and affirmation for all. When we lose that understanding, we have forsaken the message of the Bible. No matter what, use your faith as a tool to promote love, acceptance, inclusion, and equity for all, not just those who are similar to you.

THE QUEER ALLIES BIBLE

Summary: Religion and the LGBTQIA+ Community

- The Challenging Relationship Between Religion and the LGBTQIA+ Community
- Facing My Own Faith
- Christianity
- What is the problem?
- Leviticus 18:22
- 1 Cor. 6:9-11
- 1 Tim. 1:10-11
- Rom. 1:26-27
- Ps. 139:13-14
- Gen. 1:27
- Gal 3:28
- Eph. 6:5-7
- Rethinking Our Faith

12. Becoming NV

When people ask me to share the story of my transition, I typically don't know where to start. The journey has been truly beautiful—but at the same time, it has been extremely taxing. It's still hard for me to relive some details of my past, especially those from my youth. I've also made many mistakes, and made some choices about how I came out—choices I sometimes wish I could take back. However, without those experiences—both good and bad—I would not be the person I am today.

I gave a lot of thought before deciding to include my personal journey in these pages. Naturally, I haven't shared every detail of my life, as there are some things I'm not ready to make public. Still, I've chosen to include my story because I want you to learn from what I have gone through. I want you to understand my struggle for self-understanding in order to gain insight into the unique and challenging aspects of exploring sexuality or transitioning genders.

Living In The Shadows

I grew up in a white middle class suburb just north of Columbus, Ohio, with two parents who were excellent providers for my basic needs. I had a brother, plenty of pets, and extended family close by. I never really wanted for much, materially. I was an average student, and had the financial resources to play any sport or engage in any activity I chose. No matter the endeavor, my parents were there to cheer me on and motivate me to try new things. They were incredibly supportive and offered me their love. Anyone who met us would have thought that we were a happy and loving family.

We were also regular church-goers. Church provided weekly structure and spiritual education for me and my brother.

Despite all of this, from my early childhood, I felt that I couldn't be my true self, that I had to pretend to be the boy I thought my parents wanted me to be. I was taught through paternal guidance and spiritual lessons that my role was to be a man. I knew exactly what that meant! Still, I felt "wrong" being a boy, but never understood those feelings. I would often daydream about what it would be like to be a girl, or be able to express my femininity—but those thoughts were quickly followed by terrible anxiety about actually expressing myself in that way.

I feared sharing my gender questioning with my parents, as I had been taught in church and by statements made in our home that homosexuality was sinful. This caused a great deal of distress for me, and by my teen years I often became angry and emotional without really understanding why. Because of this behavior, my parents referred to me as "Hamlet"—a label I absolutely loathed.

Looking back, I now understand that my outbursts and anger were a cry for help that should have raised red flags. Later, there were attempted suicides. I ran away from home, and acted violently towards family members. All of this was explained away as me being "Hamlet." Several years of intense therapy helped me come to terms with my gender identity by guiding me through my past in order to make sense of my feelings. Today, I wish that I could show my younger self the amazing feminine individual I have become.

The Freedom to Be... ?

My first memory of questioning my gender occurred when I was eight years old, when my father took my brother and I to see *X-Men*. I wasn't a comic book fan at the time, so I had no idea what to expect. By the end of the film, my outlook on life had completely changed due to one character, Mystique. OMG! Her appearance in the film was life-altering for me as I watched her change from male to female. Shapeshifting was Mystique's super power, and after seeing *X-Men*, I wanted this power, too. I thought that it would be the simplest way to live as a girl without my parents finding out. I could mutate when no one was around and experience femininity, then transform back to male. But alas, that power doesn't exist. So, I was forced to repress what I felt.

During my childhood, questions about sexuality and gender would come up from time to time. This was especially difficult for me because of my last name. Yes, "Gay" was my surname at birth, which now is awesome! During my childhood, however, that name made life miserable, as other kids constantly questioned my sexuality. In response, I felt that I needed to appear to be the stereotypical heterosexual male—which made my secret gender questions even tougher. I publicly hid behind the facade of being male, but deep down I wished I could just talk to someone about how I felt.

At night, I prayed to live my life as a girl. I wanted to experience how I felt inside for just one day—I told myself that would be enough, and then I could just move on and be the boy I was "supposed" to be. Unfortunately, I'd wake up the next morning only to discover that my prayer hadn't been answered.

My parents were not supportive of gay people. Listening to their frequent remarks made me feel unsafe, angry, and depressed. They always told my brother and I that we could be honest with them and share our innermost thoughts. Unfortunately, their beliefs towards queer individuals told me that the opposite was true.

I was also taught that God had the answer, and that going to church would help me feel better. But that never helped because our church leaders preached that LGBTQIA+ life was sinful.

One song in particular hit close to home during those years of silent questioning—"Creep" by Radiohead. This song spoke to me in ways I did not understand until well into adulthood, after I had come out and transitioned my gender. The chorus summed up how I felt:

> *But I'm a creep /*
> *I'm a weirdo /*
> *What the hell am I doin' here? /*
> *I don't belong here*

I listened to the song over and over again, played it on my guitar, and sang my heart out, feeling that for four minutes, I could express how I truly felt on the inside. I felt like a creep. I felt "wrong" for having these feelings. Now I understand that I was neither a wrong nor a creep; I was a lost child, seeking the freedom to be who I was meant to be.

Fear Of School

After elementary school, my parents decided to homeschool me and my brother. There were many reasons for their decision, and looking back, I realize that it did actually help me. School was never easy for me due to my inability to concentrate and focus; therefore the one-on-one attention of homeschooling was beneficial. More importantly, home was a sanctuary from the mocking children, and provided me with a means to escape reality. Whenever I was not involved in schoolwork, I was in my bedroom creating Lego worlds where I could express my gender, sexuality, and personality more than I ever could in the real world.

I was homeschooled from sixth grade to the first half of eighth grade. This was extremely difficult on my mother, who had to wear many professional hats in order to provide my brother and I with the education we needed. This came to an end when my parents decided that it was time for us to return to public school. Outraged by this decision, I became angry and violent, and eventually made my way to the car in an attempt to drive away. Thankfully, a neighbor was there to stop me.

Fortunately, when I returned to public school, my worst fears didn't materialize. While the mocking did start up again, it was not nearly as bad as I had anticipated. Still, I no longer had the freedom to spend my time in fantasy worlds.

Back at school, I fell back into the routine of over-performing my masculinity in order to remain hidden from the critical gaze of others. It was not until high school that I began to express my gender identity more freely. This was all thanks to watching a school performance of *A Midsummers Night's Dream*. I fell in love with how the boys on stage could be more "feminine" and no one cared. In fact, they were all cheered at the end of the performance. I had finally found a way to experience a small portion of the person I was inside without people thinking I was gay.

The World's A Stage

Theater became a place where I could finally experience some semblance of gender freedom. All good things have to come to an end, however, and this happened during the winter of my junior year.

We were set to perform the musical *Pippin*, and I was excited. I was also finally gaining some real traction in dating the girl of my dreams—Katie, who would eventually become my wife. I auditioned for the show, and felt great about my chances to land a decent role, but when the casting list was posted, my excitement quickly turned into anger, as I was given the role of "The Bearded Lady."

My anger was not at the fact that this was a background character, but rather who the character was. As an adult, I have rocked a beard and a face full of makeup, but for a high school junior, this felt like the end of the world. I had escaped into the theater to quietly experiment with my gender—not to have it blatantly paraded on stage for everyone to see. I had finally escaped the mocking of my last name for the most part, and now it was all in jeopardy.

I approached the theater director and explained to her that I did not feel comfortable with this part, and asked to be recast. She told me that since the casting list had been made public, the entire school expected me to play the role and that I would have to accept it. I couldn't just quit, as the performance was tied to my grade in theater class. I was stuck, and I hated her. More importantly, I hated myself.

I continued with the role until one day when I was asked to step into a classroom with the director. There, she gave me a sparkling blue dress to wear for the performance, and told me to try it on to make sure it fit. I took the dress and went to the storage room, where I would be alone. I did want anyone to see me, as I was ashamed. I put the dress on and looked in the mirror, only to discover that I was sexually aroused—I experienced an intense gender euphoria. For a moment it was amazing—but my excitement was quickly replaced by hate, anger, and disgust. I ripped the dress off and put my regular clothes back on, crying from the pain I was feeling.

I went back to the director, still crying, and told her that I would not perform as the bearded lady. Now, any person with a shred of decency or empathy would have recognized the agony I was feeling. Unfortunately, that was not the case here, as I was told by the teacher me that I would appear as the bearded lady or fail the class. I left school and drove home, contemplating whether to drive off the road.

In order not to fail the class, I went ahead and played the bearded lady, giving the most half-assed performance possible, going out of my way to try and ruin the show. I wanted to hurt the director the way I had been hurt. I did just enough to make sure that I would "pass" the class, but my worst fears had been realized. Theater was no longer an escape for me.

The mockery also began again. My classmates, friends, everyone in school began calling me gay, but now adding "tranny." To escape, I threw myself into my relationship with Katie and left everything else behind. But the damage had been done, and I desperately needed to try to figure myself out. The gender euphoria I had felt wearing the dress was like a drug. I couldn't get it out of my head, feeling that I needed one more fix—yet I hated myself because of it. I can't count the number of times I considered suicide during this period.

Then Katie left to go to Ashland University, and I was alone for my senior year of high school. On Saturdays, I'd wake up at four in the morning and drive up to see Katie at college, getting there as early as possible so that I could spend the day with her. No one at her school knew of my past, and that gave me a feeling of freedom.

Eventually, I graduated from high school and followed Katie, also attending Ashland. All I wanted to do was leave the past behind.

Rebirth

Like many transgender individuals, I spent years going back and forth while experimenting with my gender. This is often referred to as a "purge." It is quite common for those who are exploring their gender identity, but have yet to come out. My experimentation was associated with sex. I felt that I could justify cross-dressing if it were part of a sexual act. Thus, I would go through periods of allowing myself to dress more feminine while engaging in sex. I would take Katie shopping for dresses and outfits, purchasing items her mother would consider "inappropriate." This gave me brief opportunities to re-experience that moment of gender euphoria—the "high" I so badly needed. Yet even with this experimentation, I felt like I still needed to keep up the facade of the heterosexual male in front of others.

In June 2014, Katie and I got married. We had just graduated from college and decided we needed a new start, so we moved to Charleston, South Carolina. Katie got a job as an elementary intervention specialist, while I became a middle school math teacher. At this point, my gender experimentation was gone. Instead, I attempted to be the perfect husband, teacher, and "man." This need for perfection was my eventual demise.

After moving back to Ohio in 2015, Katie and I spent the summer of 2016 traveling in our Subaru and camping at national parks. During this trip everything began to change. As we drove into Rocky Mountain National Park, we had one of our worst fights. I wanted to be completely open with Katie, so I finally admitted that I was questioning my gender. I couldn't explain what I meant or exactly what I wanted—just that I didn't understand my gender.

That night we survived a terrible wind storm by literally holding up our tent to prevent it from collapsing or blowing away. We also engaged in a true dialogue about what I was feeling. I still felt my gender questioning to be in a sexual manner, that maybe I was a "sissy" or a "submissive"—not what I would eventually understand my gender to actually be.

This is a very hard thing for a spouse to understand and deal with. Katie and I had to be open with each other to understand how my gender questioning and our relationship would work. To her credit, she handled it as well as anyone could, especially because I had no idea exactly what I thought my gender was at the time.

It wasn't until 2018 that I began to figure it out. That fall, I started working with a therapist—not about my gender questioning, but about my anger. The drive for male "perfection" was killing me. It would have been the end of my marriage if I hadn't sought professional help. During my sessions, I began to break down the walls I had built and to understand why I was so mad all the time. I started to see that I had repressed myself while trying to be the person that I thought others wanted me to be. Slowly, I started to understand that I needed to seek my authentic self by addressing my gender.

On December 18, 2018, I was sitting on the couch in my therapist's office and staring at the clock. I wanted to run out the hour so I could leave without addressing the voice screaming in my head. However, the screaming was so loud that it eventually burst out: "I feel like sometimes I want to be a woman!"

I got up to walk out, and my therapist said, "Sit your ass back down." We spent the next hour talking about what I meant by this. I admitted that I didn't want to be a woman completely, as I liked some parts of my male self. I said I wanted to be Mystique from *X-Men*. My therapist explained to me that my gender questioning was completely normal, and that the explanations of my gender actually aligned with being genderfluid. We then discussed how I would come out to my wife.

Later, sitting in our living room, shortly after coming out to my therapist, I came out to Katie. I cannot express how grateful I am for how well she responded. I honestly believe that she was just relieved that we finally had an understanding of my gender identity.

Eighteen years after I had first begun to question my gender, I had an identity—and someone wonderful to share it with.

The Winding Road

I actually hate the term "coming out" because it makes people think that you only do it once, and then everything's fine. In reality, LGBTQIA+ individuals are in a constant state of "coming out," as the self-discovery of their sexuality, gender, or both, is not linear. Society expects them to know exactly who they are and what they want from the moment they first come out. That expectation is horrible! No one understands exactly what they want immediately after such a huge self-discovery. It takes time and lived experience to figure things out. To determine what's right for yourself.

Coming out is a powerful process for an LGBTQIA+ individual—when it occurs properly. What do I mean by that? A person should come out on their own timetable, without being forced out because of external circumstances. Coming out to my wife was ideal because I wasn't forced to do it, and it happened when I was ready, in a safe, comfortable place.

Coming out is also a time to allow people to come into your life. Let me explain: you wouldn't let strangers walk into your house and make themselves at home. You try, instead, to determine whether or not you feel safe with them. The same is true when you allow people to be part of your sexual and gender identity. In order to share that part of your life with them, you have to trust them and believe they will accept you for who you truly are.

Allowing people to see my true gender was difficult. It went very well with Katie, which encouraged me to share my new-found gender identity with everyone who was important in my life. I began with my close friends, the ones that I had made in college and remained connected with to this day. I got everyone together and told them about my gender identity during a dinner party. I was nervous as hell—I didn't know if I would be accepted or cast aside. I was lucky enough to have been met with joy and love.

This led me to the hard step of coming out to my parents. Unfortunately, I did so in the worst possible way. Rather than entering the conversation with a plan and enough time to speak calmly, I blurted it out, catching them completely off guard. Looking back, that was a huge mistake. However, at that moment I just wanted to prove my childhood self wrong—that my parents would accept me for who I was.

The night ended without much reaction from them, which gave me hope that they might accept me. I believed they just needed time to understand what I had been going through all those years. Instead, I was eventually met with aggressive questions about my gender identity. I was caught off guard when my parents suggested that I only wear feminine clothing in other cities, and that I didn't respect how my identity would affect their lives. They claimed to be concerned about my safety, but they were actually concerned that they would be seen by their colleagues and friends as the parents of a "tranny."

Over the next year, they criticized me for not having a set plan for my future, and often attacked me for my gender and sexual exploration. I persisted, still wanting to prove my younger self wrong. I wanted the unconditional love that my parents had always said they would give me. There were moments that gave me hope, such as when my mother invited me to go clothes shopping with her. However, one night changed my relationship with them forever.

It was late January 2020, right before COVID-19 shut down the world. I had invited my parents to my house for dinner and drinks, hoping that after a good meal we could discuss our relationship. I told them that I wanted them to see me as their daughter—the person that I'd always been. I asked them to respect and use my lived name, correct pronouns, and affirm my identity. My parents refused, and told me that I could only be their son.

Their refusal to affirm my gender identity devastated me. At first I was unable to speak or move, leaving Katie the responsibility of removing them from our home. Than I went manic and lost all control. What I remember are bits and pieces of that night. Several times, I tried to get a gun to use on myself; thankfully Katie didn't allow that to happen. I eventually got on the phone with an emergency suicide prevention counselor from The Trevor Project, and was led out of my home by police officers who took me to the local hospital and a mental heath facility.

The time I spent in the mental health facility was extremely frightening, and something I hope never to repeat, but it was necessary. My hospitalization gave me the chance for the self-reflection I needed to gain control of my mental health. I needed to focus on what would make me happiest—not how I wanted others to see me. I had come out because I wanted to be able to fully express my gender identity, but I was still living for how I wanted people to see me. I wanted my parents to accept me so badly that I refused to acknowledge that it was not going to happen. It was not until I had reached rock bottom that I understood that it wasn't my job to make them understand and accept me. If they were going to do so, it would have to be something that they did on their own. I had to live for myself, within my gender identity.

Living An Authentic Life

After leaving the mental health facility, I cut ties with my parents as well as anyone else who did not accept me. My guilt about my parents later made me try to reconcile with them, as I believed that I had to be the "bigger person" and accept them for who they were, even if they wouldn't accept me for who I was. This began a cycle of attempts to rebuild our relationship, only to have it end as it had before. At one point, I received a message from my mother telling me that I should be grateful to them for giving me life. This caused me a great deal of turmoil, and led me to finally tell my parents that I didn't want any contact with them unless they were willing to accept me fully and love me unconditionally. Almost five years after first coming out to them, I had finally stood up for myself.

While I don't currently have a relationship with my biological parents, I do have a deep kinship with my chosen family. My chosen mother found me at my lowest point and took me in as her own. She gifted me her *Tallit*, a Jewish prayer shawl. The *Tallit* is worn to create a sense of communion with God during prayer. While I am not Jewish, this gift means the world to me. I honor her heritage and respect the customs of her family in gratitude for everything she has done for me. Every time I wrap myself in her *Tallit* I feel the unconditional love and support she offers me—exactly what I have always longed for.

I sometimes find myself missing my childhood relationship with my parents. I long to develop an adult mother-daughter relationship with my mother and have my father recognize my unique beauty, and to receive their unconditional love for who I am, not who they want me to be. People change and grow, so I leave the door open for them—and others—to re-enter my life when they are ready to accept and affirm me. However, they must understand that I will not compromise my identity in order to repair my relationships. It took me many years to accept who I am—and I want others to respect that process. The choice is theirs. Even allies may be faced with having to distance themselves from those who withhold respect for their LGBTQIA+ loved ones.

Transitioning

My path to transitioning was filled with many challenges. When I first came out in 2018, I understood myself to be a genderfluid cross-dresser. At the time, I believed I would express my gender fluidity sparingly and spend most of my time in a masculine expression. As I allowed my gender fluidity to develop, I realized that I was not comfortable with expressing my feminine self only on occasion.

During the early years of my transition, I attempted to understand my gender through sexual fantasies, believing that was the only authentic way for me to express my femininity. In time I understood that this was not the best way for me to express my gender. During the COVID-19 pandemic I began to allow myself to truly live as the person I was meant to be.

As I embraced myself, I worked with a team of affirming doctors who were able to help me determine exactly what I needed. It is common for LGBTQIA+ individuals to have a team of doctors and therapists who support their growth from a social to a medical transition. The "traditional" path is to begin with hormone replacement therapy (HRT) for at least a year before beginning surgical procedures. However, this was not my path. Instead, my doctors and therapists helped me gain an awareness that what I was missing most were breasts. As a kid I constantly thought about my chest, and felt that a weight was missing from my body, that I was not "complete." When I wore breast forms early in my transition, I could feel what I'd been lacking.

I eventually came to understand that breast forms were not enough. After I discussed this with my medical team, we determined that I needed breast enhancement surgery. As I mentioned earlier in the book, I was denied my first scheduled surgery a week before the operation. Later I was grateful to have the procedure performed at the Cleveland Clinic by Dr. Raymond Isakov. While Dr. Isakov is a cisgender man, he provided me with attentive care throughout the phases of my surgery. Instead of simply telling me what he was going to do, he listened to my questions and helped me understand the process.

One of the best things Dr. Isakov did happened before the surgery. When I was wheeled into the operating room, he greeted me and told me to look at the stack of boxes to my right. He explained that the boxes contained a selection of breast implants. Instead of just picking a size and conducting the operation, he was going to "try out" different sizes to see what would fit best with my body. This showed the level of professionalism Dr. Isakov brought to my care. Since the operation, I have experienced a sense of wholeness with my body.

While I didn't feel the need for additional surgeries, I needed to receive HRT before I was mentally at peace. HRT helped me manage my emotions so that I finally attained physical and mental completion.

Understanding What You Lose...And What You Gain

Transitioning genders involves a lot of twists and turns, and obstacles that seem unpassable at the time. It leads us in unexpected directions. At times the journey is extremely difficult. In the end, however, it is all worth it!

I lost a lot while transitioning. I lost my job as a teacher and coach. I lost friends. I lost my family—and my wife's family as well. And I lost myself for a time. People fear coming out because they think they'll lose everything they've built. Yes, it sometimes happens. Unfortunately, due to the pressures presented by our heteronormative and cisnormative culture, loss is to be expected. However, you can turn that loss into something positive. I felt a great sense of loss when I left my positions as a teacher and a coach. Now, I apply those skills to inspire others. I teach allies to be inclusive and affirming. I am a sought-after and accomplished photographer, with my work shown all over the globe. I have become the person I had always aspired to be, though my journey was different from the one I expected. Not only am I able to help many people, but I still connect with my former students, who now see me as their lifelong teacher, not just their sixth grade math instructor!

We now come to the present, and the beautiful queer person I have become. I am married to an incredible woman who has stood beside me since high school. I have three fur babies I love very much, and a chosen family that affirms me fully. I would have never gotten here without taking that first step—choosing to express my true self, rather than trying to please everyone else. My childhood prayers have been answered, as I am living as I was always meant to be! My body and my gender identity finally align, and everything just feels right.

I hope to one day see a world where every LGBTQIA+ person can live authentically. I also hope that in reading this book, you now have a greater understanding and appreciation for the LGBTQIA+ community, and that this motivates you to become the ally the community needs.

You are beautiful and deserve to live authentically. Never allow anyone to tell you otherwise.

This is Trans
a photographic journey of awareness and love

"This is Trans" is a photography project I started in 2022 to break down the stigmas that continue to plague the transgender community, and to bring together the incredible diversity that being transgender represents.

"Transgender" is often mistakenly thought of as a binary concept in which a person must transition from one gender to the other—male to female, or female to male. In truth, "trans" simply means that an individual identifies differently than the gender/sex they were assigned at birth.

Another mistaken belief is that a transgender person is only valid if they transition fully with the use of hormone replacement therapy and gender confirming surgeries. While some transgender individuals transition in this way, the goal of "This is Trans" is to show that "transgender" covers an array of identities, each of which is unique, beautiful, and fully valid. Several participants joined this project because they had been told that they were not genuinely transgender because they had not transitioned socially and medically from one binary gender to the other.

Along with their portrait, participants were asked the following question: "What does being transgender mean to you?" Their answers are shown beneath their portrait, along with the person's pronouns. The participants are unnamed to ensure their privacy and security.

(She/Her)

"Being trans to me means being authentic to your identity regardless of how difficult and hard it may be. We are beautiful regardless of how society treats us. We are resilient and will not be silenced."

He/Him)
"For me, being trans means being my most authentic self and recognizing myself when I look in the mirror."

(She/Her)

"Being transgender is embracing the most beautiful, difficult, and complex parts of being human. We uniquely connect to the world through expression, vulnerability, and honesty."

(They/Them)

"Being trans to me means expressing myself in a way that is true to how I feel and who I am. Having the confidence to be the human and trans role model that I desperately needed when I was younger."

(She/Her)
"Being transgender means living with fewer masks. It means not hurting myself to make other people more comfortable."

(She/Her)

"Being transgender for me mostly means exhilaration. My brief and rare moments of terror are precipitated by outside forces who refuse to understand my identity. For this reason, being transgender must necessarily be political, but fighting for a good cause enhances the exhilaration. My trans ancestors risked near constant terror to give me my opportunity for exhilaration in the present day. I hope our generation of the trans family can rise to meet this politically fraught moment to allow the next generation of trans children to understand their trans-ness with unprecedented serenity. My wish is for everyone to recognize the responsibility and privilege of individuality as sacred and nonpolitical."

(She/Her)

"Transgender, Gender Non-Conforming, and NonBinary (TGNCNB) people demonstrate that humans have the power to grow and change. Even in defiance of systems that tell us we cannot change, even in the face of exclusion, denigration, and discrimination, we can change. Isn't that a beautiful gift?"

(Xe/Xem)

"I am myself. I allow my self-expression to be fluid and thus find joy in expressing the multifaceted dynamism inherent in being a human spirit. "Neuroqueer" and "autiegender" are words I use to describe my neurodivergent queer experience. I feel whole when I recognize these identities that didn't have names for so long, parts I knew were there but didn't have words for. Being my enby self expands my joy! I surrender the pressure to 'fit in' or match the expectations of strangers and others set on misunderstanding me. My joy matters. My identity matters."

(He/Him)

"Being true to myself, full expression, self love, self acceptance, peace, the ability to move forward with confidence and see my life more clearly and allowing others to do the same."

(She/Her)

"It's a process of understanding myself, an exercise in risk and reward, being prepared for the unexpected, aligning the body and soul. I am blessed to be part of this community."

(They/Them)

"My transness is not defined by what I look like, what body parts I do or don't have, or how I have transitioned. My transness is fluid, like watercolors blending into each other across a canvas. It is feminine, masculine, and entirely neither all at once. It is pink and blue and purple and orange and yellow blending into a beautiful sun-kissed glow. Being trans means that I am allowed to have control over my own life, as is—or at least should—everyone else. It means freedom, joy, overcoming adversity. It means discovering pieces of myself, broken and unbroken, every day. Being trans means supporting others in experiencing and living their transness. It means stepping in and stepping up when myself and my trans and intersex siblings can't access the healthcare or the basic human rights we need to survive. It means teaching others about transness and fostering empathy. Being trans means community. It means hope. It means a chance at living."

(They/She/He)

"Being transgender means to be fully me, flowing through the genders that we all have known and still are getting familiar with."

(He/They)

"It's spiritual. It's everything and nothing. It frees me and binds me. Being transgender is the way I live my life- way more than an identity and label. My life started under my transgender identity. Though I believe it isn't for me. My energy is what makes me trans, but that definition is for my community. I exist for my community. I exist for our rights and health."

(She/Her)

"Being trans is admitting a belief in magic. it's more than just the clothes and the statement, it's the acknowledgment and the awareness that YOU were meant to be more than what you were born, more than the name others gave you, more than expectations and goals... and dreams that were not your own. Being trans is ripping yourself free from the ties holding you to a place you never felt truly comfortable. It's a sense of warmth and comfort now knowing that the little voice in the back of your head wasn't lying, it wasn't hurting you. It was telling you to run towards your gut feeling and let yourself be true. There is only one you that's you, so why not be the truest you there ever was?"

(She/Fae)

"I see my gender as the burst of light that encompasses a firework. A sudden bright light that makes you feel a sense of awe, and wonder. My gender is magic."

(She/Her)

"Being transgender to me is being able to express who I am on the inside. It is me not identifying with the labels given to me at birth and instead taking that power back and identifying myself for who I am. Being Transgender is more than an identity for me though. Coming out as a transgender woman is what gave me my voice back. It gave me the happiness I need in order to enjoy my life. It is what saved me."

(They/He)

"For me, being trans is sacred; a calling. It's a journey of trust and uncertainty, yet so unfathomably beautiful. I trust in God (they/she/any) to give me the strength to fight for justice and equity in this world, especially for my queer siblings.

I service and build pipe organs for a living. I love doing anything hands-on, especially as I've noticed my body changing. I know it sounds weird, but sometimes when I can't connect to my body, I come back by soldering some metal or picking up some lumber. It helps bring me back into myself. Each day I meet and engage with new people and places. For a lot of people, it's their first time seeing someone like me. I see part of this as my mission. I am just one small person in this big world, but I believe that just one person can make a difference.

I come from a past of immense religious trauma, but ironically enough, it was clergy that helped me grow into myself. I am a member of the Christian Church (Disciples of Christ) in Ohio. I watched as our denomination voted at the General Assembly this year to unanimously and unequivocally affirm my trans and gender-diverse siblings and actively oppose anti-trans legislation. Now, I am in seminary, studying to be a minister, to turn back around and help my siblings who are recovering from religious trauma. Is it to make them religious? Absolutely not. That is just how I am comfortable in myself—my religion is very personal. However, if I can be a hand to hold on to, a person to cry with, a sibling to stand in as family, and an academic to study those cliche biblical "slam" verses to tell my siblings that it's the hateful homophobes and transphobes that have no place in Christianity? That is, God (they/she/any) willing, who I hope to be."

ALLY RESOURCES

LGBTQIA+ Pioneers

This list includes important LGBTQIA+ pioneers who used their voices and platforms to advocate for the community.

Marsha P. Johnson (1945 – 1992)

One of the most prominent LGBTQIA+ activists, famously known for throwing the first brick during the Stonewall Riots.

Harvey Milk (1930 - 1978)

First openly gay elected politician in the United States.

RuPaul Charles (1960 - present)

Considered to be the most commercially famous drag queen, and creator of the iconic television competition show, *RuPaul's Drag Race*.

James Baldwin (1924 - 1987)

Writer and activist best known for his works on the state of race and discrimination with the African American and LGBTQIA+ communities.

Christine Jorgensen (1926 - 1989)

WWII veteran, actress, and singer who became famous for being the first openly transgender woman to have sex reassignment surgery.

Billie Jean King (1943 - present)

A pioneer for equality and the inclusion of women and LGBTQIA+ people in sports.

Gilbert Baker (1951 - 2017)

American artist, best known as the creator of the Rainbow Pride Flag.

Laverne Cox (1972 - present)

Pioneering transgender actress and activist best known for her groundbreaking role in the Netflix series *Orange is the New Black*.

Audre Lorde (1934 - 1992)

The warrior poet, famous for her incredible works advocating for women's rights, the Civil Rights Movement, and LGBTQIA+ rights.

Larry Kramer (1935 - 2020)

American playwright, author, film director, and LGBTQIA+ activist. Founder of the AIDS Coalition to Unleash Power (ACT UP).

Stormé DeLarverie (1920 - 2014)

Legendary drag king performer and LGBTQIA+ activist. Best known for throwing the first punch during the Stonewall Riots.

Jim Obergefell (1966 - present)

American LGBTQIA+ activist who was the plaintiff in the 2015 Supreme Court case *Obergefell vs. Hodges* which legalized same sex marriages across the United States.

Lana Wachowski (1965 - present) and Lilly Wachowski (1967 - present)

Sisters who created the *Matrix* film franchise; both transgender women.

Alan Turing (1912 - 1954)

British mathematician, credited for breaking the German enigma code during WWII. Was chemically castrated after coming out as gay and died of cyanide poisoning from the castration.

Willi Ninja (1961 - 2006)

Known as the grandfather of Vogue, a popular dance form of queer night clubs and balls. Featured prominently in the documentary, *Paris is Burning*.

Lorraine Vivian Hansberry (1930 - 1965)

First African American female author to have a play performed on Broadway.

Jackie Shane (1940 - 2019)

Transgender American soul singer in Nashville and Toronto. Her album, *Any Other Way*, won a Grammy in 2019 for Best Historical Album.

Roberta Cowell (1918 - 2011)

Britsh transwoman fighter pilot in World War II, and professional race car driver. Was one of the first people to undergo gender confirmation surgery, receiving one of the first successful vaginoplasty surgeries in 1951.

Sarah McBride (1990 - president)

First transgender person elected to Congress. Elected to represent Delaware At-Large District in the United States House of Representatives.

Miss Major Griffin-Gracy (1940 - present)

Transgender activist who was on the frontlines of the Stonewall Riots. Was the executive director of the Transgender Gender Variant Intersex Justice Project.

King James VI and I (1566 - 1625)

Former King of England, known to be the most prominent homosexual figure in the early modern period. Known for the King James Version of the Christian Bible.

Bruce Voeller (1934 - 1994)

Biologist and gay-rights activists who coined the term AIDS (Acquired Immune Deficiency Syndrome) to counter homophobic names for the disease. Co-founder of the National Gay Task Force.

Mary Yu (1957 - present)

Washington State Supreme Court Justice. First Latina, Asian-American, and open gay justice.

Recommended Reading List

Below is a list of books I highly recommend. Each title focuses on a different area of the LGBTQIA+ community, providing you with the education and tools to become an even more effective ally.

Early Childhood

And Tango Makes Three by Peter Parnell, Justin Richardson, and Henry Cole

Being You: A First Conversation About Gender by Megan Madison, Jessica Ralli, and Anne/Andy Passchier

My Shadow is Purple by Scott Stuart

Gender Identity for Kids by Anne/Andy Passchier

Téo's Tutu by Maryann Jacob Macias, and Alea Marley

Elementary

10,000 Dresses by Marcus Ewert and Rex Ray

Call Me Max by Kyle Lukoff and Luciano Lozano

Calvin by Vanessa Ford and JR Ford

A Child's Introduction to Pride: The Inspirational History and Culture of the Lgbtqia+ Community by Sarah Prager and Caitlin O'Dwyer

It Feels Good to Be Yourself: A Book about Gender Identity by Theresa Thorn and Noah Grigni

Mama and Mommy and Me in the Middle by Nina Lacour and Kaylani Juanita

My Rainbow by DeShanna Neal and Trinity Neal

Twas the Night Before Pride by Joanna McClintick and Juana Medina

Payden's Pronoun Party by Blue Jaryn and Xochitl Cornejo

Middle School

Different Kinds of Fruit by Kyle Lukoff
The Many Half-Lived Lives of Sam Sylvester by Maya MacGregor
The Other Boy by M. G. Hennessey
Pet by Akwaeke Emezi
The Civil War of Amos Abernathy by Michael Leali

Young Adult

All Boys Aren't Blue: A Memoir-Manifesto by George M. Johnson

The 57 Bus: A True Story of Two Teenagers and the Crime That Changed Their Lives by Dashka Slater

GLBTQ: The Survival Guide for Gay, Lesbian, Bisexual, Transgender, and Questioning Teens by Kelly Huegel Madrone

She/He/They/Me : For the Sisters, Misters, and Binary Resisters by Robyn Ryle

A Queer History of the United States for Young People by Michael Bronski, Adapted by Richie Chevat

Our Work Is Everywhere: An Illustrated Oral History of Queer and Trans Resistance by Syan Rose

Am I Blue?: Coming Out from the Silence by Marion Dane Bauer and Beck Underwood

Almost Perfect by Brian Katcher

Growing Up Gay/Lesbian: A Literary Anthology by Bennett L. Singer

The Miseducation of Cameron Post by Emily M. Danforth

Man o' War by Cory McCarthy

Queer: The Ultimate LGBT Guide for Teens by Kathy Belge, Marke Bieschke, and Christian Robinson

Adult

The Little Book of LGBTQ+: An A-Z of Gender and Sexual Identities by Harriet Dyer

Gay Parents/Straight Schools: Building Communication and Trust by Virginia Casper and Steven B. Schultz

I Am Ace by Cody Diagle-Orians

The Ace and Aro Relationship Guide: Making It Work in Friendship, Love, and Sex by Cody Diagle-Orians

The Transgender Child: Revised & Updated Edition: A Handbook for Parents and Professionals Supporting Transgender and Nonbinary Children by Stephanie Brill and Rachel Pepper

Families Like Mine: Children of Gay Parents Tell It Like It Is by Abigail Garner

Transgender History: The Roots of Today's Revolution by Susan Stryker

Tomorrow Will Be Different: Love, Loss, and the Fight for Trans Equality by Sarah McBride

A Quick and Easy Guide to Neopronouns by D. F. Koz, Esq.

Sissy: A Coming-of-Gender Story by Jacob Tobia

Queer Conception by Kristin Liam Kali

Inverse Cowgirl: A Memoir by Alicia Weigel

Becoming Nicole by Amy Ellis Nutt

The Gospel of Inclusion: A Christian Case for LGBT+ Inclusion in the Church by Brandon Robertson

Queer & Christian: Reclaiming the Bible, Our Faith, and Our Place at the Table by Brandon Robertson

Pageboy: A Memoir by Elliot Page

Gender: Your Guide: A Gender-Friendly Primer on What to Know, What to Say, and What to Do in the New Gender Culture by Lee Airton

A Quick & Easy Guide to They/Them Pronouns by Archie Bongiovanni and Tristan Jimerson

The Educator's Guide to LGBT+ Inclusion by Kryss Shane

Beyond the Gender Binary by Alok Vaid-Menon and Ashley Lukashevsky

Walking the Bridgeless Canyon by Kathy Baldock

Included in Christ by Cristy Perdue, MD

Recommended Media List

These powerful and insightful films and television shows will help you understand the challenges faced by the LGBTQIA+ community. For the most part, realistic representations of LGBTQIA+ individuals in cinema and television have been rare.

Discloser
Showcases the homophobic and transphobic history and misrepresentation of LGBTQIA+ individuals in film and television.

Moonlight
The story of a young Black man growing up and understanding his sexuality while living in an extremely homophobic culture.

Paris Is Burning
Documents the ballroom scene in New York City durings the 1980's and 1990's.

The Fallout
High school girls navigating significant trauma and exploring their sexuality.

The Death and Life of Marsha P. Johnson
An examination of the life and controversial death of the pioneering transgender activist.

Pose
A television drama showcasing the icons and legends of ballroom culture in New York City, and the LGBTQ subculture in the African-American and Latino communities during the 1980s.

Will and Harper
A powerful documentary focusing on the friendship of Will Ferrell and Harper Steele as they embark on a road trip to help Harper find her place within the society she once loved.

Schitt's Creek
A television series focusing on the trials and tribulations of a family who lost their wealth and had to begin again. Expertly showcases many representations of sexuality.

1946: The Mistranslation that Shifted A Culture
A documentary showcasing the mistranslation that occurred around the first known case of the word homosexual, and the damage that mistranslation caused.

How to Survive A Plague
A powerful documentary exploring the lives of those who lived through the AIDS epidemic and the advocates who played a huge role in providing education to reduce the number of AIDS-related deaths.

Every Body
The stories of three intersex individuals who overcome childhood traumas and non-consensual medical procedures to become thriving adults.

Mama Bears

An exploration of the path two advocates known as "mama bears" took in order to transform their love for LGBTQIA+ children into love for the entire community.

Out North: MNLGBTQ History
This documentary history of Minnesota's LGBTQIA+ community since the 1970s.

Gender Affirming Resources

In the early stages of their gender transition, many individuals use gender-affirming clothing and other items to decrease their dysphoria and express their gender identity. These include binders, breast forms, gaffs, packers, and more. Oftentimes, these items are used to help a transgender individual determine whether they wish to progress to medicinal or surgical interventions.

Gender-affirming gear and items should be used correctly to avoid self-harm. Breast binding, for example, is something that a transgender individual assigned female at birth might do to attain a more masculine appearance. This can be extremely dangerous if done incorrectly, especially if duct tape or medical tape are used instead of a binder. Similarly, genital tucking by an individual assigned male at birth can be harmful without the use of gender-affirming items, such as gaffs.

Here is a list of highly recommended organizations and companies that provide safe and effective gender-affirming gear. You can also check with your local LGBTQIA+ centers and nonprofit organizations, as they may be able to provide these items for your LGBTQIA+ loved ones.

Plume Clinic (https://getplume.co). Offers virtual and affordable gender-affirming care throughout most of the United States.

Transguy Supply (https://transguysupply.com). Female to male stand to pee (STP) prosthetics and devices, packers, and clothing.

For Them (https://www.forthem.com). Providers of

tucking undergarments and binders.

Trans Essentials (https://www.ftmessentials.com). Female to male transgender gender-affirming gear including packers, binders, gaffs, and more.

UNTAG (https://untag.com). Gender-affirming swimwear, clothing, underwear, prosthetics, tucking gear, and more. Made for all bodies.

Unclockable (https://unclockable.com). Male to female transgender tucking kits and breast forms.

Origami Customs (https://origamicustoms.com). Gender-affirming swimwear and underwear for transgender individuals of all sizes.

Gender Gear (https://www.gendergear.ca). A Canadian company providing packers, gaffs, tucking underwear, binders, breast forms, and more.

Point of Pride (https://www.pointofpride.org). Organization providing free binders and shapewear, as well as funds for transgender gender-affirming care.

TransTape (https://transtape.life). A gender-affirming, body transformation system that's a backless and waterproof alternative to bras, binders, packers, gaffes, and other self-affirming products.

LeoLines (https://www.etsy.com/shop/leolines). Colorful, high quality, handmade swimwear designed to be worn without the need for tucking.

Tomboy X (https://tomboyx.com.) Provides binders, tucking underwear, and other gender-affirming clothing.

Superfit Hero (https://superfithero.com). Gender-neutral athletic wear for sizes L-7X.

The Breast Form Store (https://thebreastformstore.
com). Male to female transgender breast form inserts,
breastplates, shapewear, and other items.

Glossary of Terms

Allyship: The act of working to end oppression through support of, and as an advocate for, a group other than one's own.

Closeted: Or being "in the closet," describes people in the LGBTQIA+ community who don't publicly or openly share their sexual identity, sexual attraction, sexual behavior, gender expression, or gender identity. Some people may be out in certain communities but closeted in others due to fear of discrimination, mistreatment, rejection, or violence.

Cisgender (not trans): Those whose gender identities, presentations, and behavior "match" (according to the gender binary and sex stereotyping) the sex they were assigned at birth. Sometimes shortened to cis.

Cisnormativity: Attitudes and behaviors that incorrectly assume gender is binary, ignoring genders besides women and men.

Chosen Name / Lived Name: A name (often a first name) that someone uses that differs from their legal/birth name. Some trans and nonbinary people may use a chosen name to affirm their gender identity. "Preferred name" has also been used, however it has been largely replaced by chosen name. "Preferred name" suggests that using someone's chosen name is optional, which can lead to deadnaming.

Coming Out: A phrase that refers to the process of being open about one's sexuality and gender. For many LGBTQIA+ people, "coming out" isn't a one-time event but a social process.

Cross-dressing: Describes a person who dresses, at least partially, as a member of a gender other than their assigned sex;
244

carries no implications of sexual orientation or gender identity.

Transvestite: An outdated term used to describe a person who engages in cross-dressing. This is considered a derogatory term by many within the LGBTQIA+ community, and is one that has historically been used to describe trans individuals as having a medical or mental disorder.

Deadnaming: Calling someone by their birth/legal name after they have changed their name. This term is often associated with trans people who have changed their name as part of their transition (coming out).

Drag: The theatrical performance of one or multiple genders while dressing in the clothing of a different gender, or in a manner different from how one would usually dress. Drag is a form of gender expression and is not an indication of gender identity.

Drag Queen: Performers who perform and act distinctly in feminine attire and expression. These performers can be of any gender.

Drag King: Performers who perform and act in distinctly masculine attire and expression. These performers can be of any gender.

Gender-Affirming Health Care: Care that holistically attends to trans and nonbinary people's physical, mental, and social health needs while respectfully affirming their gender identity. It can include gender-affirming surgery. Sometimes gender-affirming surgery is medically referred to as Gender Confirmation Surgery (GCS) or Sex Reassignment Surgery (SRS), but these are not always the preferred terms.

Gender Dysphoria: This is both a medical diagnosis and an informal term used to communicate the challenging feelings or distress people experience in relation to gender. The medical diagnosis of gender dysphoria refers to a conflict between someone's assigned sex at birth (as male, female, or intersex) and their gender identity.

Gender Euphoria: A euphoric feeling often experienced when one's gender is recognized and respected by others, when one's body aligns with one's gender, or when someone expresses themselves in accordance with their gender. Focusing on gender euphoria instead of gender dysphoria shifts focus towards the positive aspects of being transgender or gender expansive.

Gender Identity: Internal sense of being male, female, both, neither, or other gender(s).

Gender Expression: How we outwardly express our gender identity, including clothing, hair style, etc.

Gender Nonconforming: People who do not subscribe to societal expectations of typical gender expressions or roles. The term is more commonly used to refer to gender expression, how one behaves, acts, and presents themselves to others, as opposed to gender identity, which is one's internal sense of self.

Heteronormative: The concept that heterosexuality is the preferred or normal mode of sexual orientation. It assumes the gender binary and that sexual and marital relations are most fitting between people of opposite sex.

Homophobia: Oppression, discrimination, and hatred directed toward members of the LGBTQIA+ community.

Intersex: A person with a less common combination of hormones, chromosomes, and/or anatomy that are used to assign sex at birth. There are many different ways to be intersex, including conditions such as Klinefelter Syndrome, Androgen Insensitivity Syndrome, and Congenital Adrenal Hyperplasia.

Intersectionality: A term coined by law professor Kimberlé

Crenshaw in the 1980s to describe the way that multiple systems of oppression interact in the lives of those with multiple marginalized identities. Intersectionality allows us to analyze social problems more fully, shape more effective interventions, and promote more inclusive advocacy amongst marginalized communities.

LGBTQIA+: Lesbian, Gay, Bisexual, Transgender, Queer, Intersex, Asexual, and +, meaning all others not encompassed by the acronym. This is the standard acronym used by the community.

LGBTQQIP2SAA: The updated 2023 full acronym for the community, covering most of the identities: Lesbian, Gay, Bisexual, Transgender, Queer, Questioning, Intersex, Pansexual, Two-spirit, Asexual, and Ally

Microaggressions: Brief and subtle behaviors, whether intentional or not, that communicate hostile, derogatory, or negative messages about commonly oppressed identities. These actions cause harm through the invalidation of the oppressed person's identity, and may reinforce stereotypes.

Misgender: Calling someone a word that does not reflect their gender. This could be a pronoun such as he/her or a form of address such as ladies/guys. This may be unintentional and without ill intent or can be an intentional expression of discrimination.

Neopronouns: Gender-neutral pronouns such as ze/zir or ey/em that are used instead of more traditional ones such as they/them.

Neurodivergent: Means having a brain that works differently from the "neurotypical" person. This may include differences in social preferences, ways of learning, ways of communicating, and/or ways of perceiving the environment.

Passing: When a trans individual is perceived as, or "passes" as, a cisgender man or woman. Passing is often thought of as a form of privilege, and the concept can also place unrealistic or unwanted expectations on trans/nonbinary folks to conform to cisnormativity. Passing can also refer to gay/lesbian/queer people being regarded as straight. Historically, passing was often necessary as a form of safety for LGBTQIA+ individuals.

Pronouns: Linguistic tools used to refer to someone in the third person. Examples are they/them/theirs, ze/hir/hirs, she/her/hers, he/him/his. In English and some other languages, pronouns have been tied to gender and are a common area of misgendering.

QPOC/QTPOC/QTBIPOC: Queer People of Color; Queer Trans People of Color; Queer Trans Black Indigenous People of Color.

Queer: An umbrella term used to describe gender/sexual/romantic orientations or identities that fall outside of societal norms. Historically, queer has been used as an epithet/slur against the LGBTQIA+ community. Some people have reclaimed the word and self-identify in opposition to assimilation. This reclamation is a celebration of not fitting into social norms. Not all people who identify as LGBTQIA+ use "queer" to describe themselves. For example, those of earlier generations are typically averse to self-identifying in this way. The term is often considered hateful when used by those who do not identify as LGBTQIA+.

Questioning: The process of exploring one's own gender identity, gender expression, and/or sexual orientation.

Sex Assigned At Birth: Assignment and classification of people as male, female, or intersex, often based solely on physical anatomy at birth and/or karyotyping.

AFAB—Assigned Female at Birth

AMAB—Assigned Male at Birth

TGNCNB+: Refers to transgender, gender non-conforming, nonbinary, and more.

Transgender (not cis): An umbrella term to describe those whose gender identity differs from the sex they were assigned at birth. Sometimes shortened to trans. There are many ways to be trans.

Nonbinary (nonbinary): Not just male or female. Can be both an umbrella term and a specific gender identity. "Enby" is a term that refers to nonbinary individuals.

TGNCNB+: Refers to transgender, gender non-conforming, nonbinary, and more.

Transsexual: Someone who experiences a gender identity that does not align with their assigned sex at birth, and desires to permanently transition to the sex with which they identify, usually with medical assistance (including gender-affirming therapies, such as hormone replacement therapy and gender-affirming surgery) to help them align their body with their identified sex. Transexual falls under the transgender umbrella, but can have mixed meanings. According to the APA (American Psychological Association) Style Guide, the term "transsexual" is largely outdated, but some people identify with it; this term should be used only for an individual who specifically claims it.

Transphobia: Deeply rooted negative beliefs about what it means to be transgender, nonbinary, and gender nonconforming.

Acknowledgments

I would like to take this opportunity to give credit to the incredible individuals who made this book possible.

Carly Jones, who was the first person to step up and help me collect my thoughts and provide a framework for this book.

Jordyn Rees Evans, Matt Reese, and Diane Hunter, who provided feedback early on in the process.

Zoe Stoller, Reverend Brandan Robertson, David Hayward, and Cody Daigle-Orians, who all provided blurbs for the book.

I must also thank the people who provided powerful and inspirational narratives on their gender/sexual identities, along with the obstacles they have overcome.

I want to acknowledge my publisher, Robert Lasner of Ig Publishing, who took a chance on me when no one else would. He saw the true impact and need for this book, where others only saw controversy. Without him, this book would still be stuck in limbo.

To Reverend Amy Aspey and Rabbi Ari Jun, who provided insights into their beliefs.

To Reverend Dr. Ben Huelskamp, who's friendship has meant everything to me. A man who has spent many an hour debating religious philosophy, and challenging me to push the boundaries of belief and understanding.

To Reverend Marcus Atha, who spent hours working with me to rediscover my faith, and aided me in understanding that I am loved and accepted by The Creator.

To my chosen mother, Debrah Pohlot, who has aided me during my lowest points and guided me throughout my journey. She picked me up and brought me into her life when I was lost. Without her unconditional love, I would not have had the strength to create this book.

A special acknowledgment must be given to the woman who stepped up at the eleventh hour to provide editing suggestions to the book, Dr. Heather Neff. Without her expertise and insights, this book would not be as powerful and impactful.

Finally, my wife, and best friend, Katie Gay. The woman who stood beside me through everything. My high school sweetheart, the love of my life, my teacher in femininity, my everything. I love you, forever and ever!

Notes

1. Be Respectful

1. New Jersey Women Lawyer Association, "NJWLA Mourns the Loss of Justice Sandra Day O'Conner," https://www.njwla.org/njwla-mourns-the-loss-of-justice-sandra-day-oconnor/.

2. Jeffrey Jones, "LGBT Identification in U.S. Ticks up to 7.1%," Gallup, February 17, 2022, https://news.gallup.com/poll/389792/lgbt-identification-ticks-up.aspx.

3. Sharita Gruberg, Lindsay Mahowald, and John Halpin, "The State of the LGBTQ Community in 2020," Center for American Progress, October 6, 2020, https://www.americanprogress.org/article/state-lgbtq-community-2020/.

4. Elana Redfield, Kerith Conron, and Christy Mallory, "Youth Impacted by Anti-Transgender Legislation in 2024, " 2024, The Williams Institute: UCLA, https://williamsinstitute.law.ucla.edu/wp-content/uploads/2024-Anti-Trans-Legislation-Apr-2024.pdf.

5. Jessica Xing and Paula Newton, "Canada Warns LGBTQ Residents of the Risks of Traveling to the US due to Some State Laws, " CNN, August 31, 2023, https://www.cnn.com/2023/08/31/americas/canada-lgbtq-us-travel-advisory/index.html.

6. Human Rights Campaign, Resources: Laws & Legislation, "The Equality Act," Human Rights Campaign, last modified June 22, 2023, https://www.hrc.org/resources/equality.

7. Idid.

2. Learn

1. Matt Mithcell, "On Freaks and Geeks and Finding My Voice: How Pop Culture Shaped My Poetry," Literary Hub, July

22, 2021, https://lithub.com/freaks-and-geeks-and-finding-my-voice-how-pop-culture-shaped-my-poetry/.

2. Kirsty Lang, "Eddie Redmayne's Cabaret Gamble: 'I Lie in Bed Going through Routines in My Head,'" *The Times*, November 21, 2021, https://www.thetimes.co.uk/article/eddie-redmaynes-cabaret-gamble-i-lie-in-bed-going-through-routines-in-my-head-q6zxm8ld6.

3. Trans Legislation Tracker, "2023 anti-trans legislation," Translegislation.com, https://translegislation.com/bills/2023.

4. IA Legis, HS 649, 90th Gen. Assem., 2023-2024, https://legiscan.com/IA/text/HSB649/id/2911766

5. Reed, Erin, "Republicans Are Redefining the Word 'Equal' in an Iowa Anti-Trans Bill," *The Guardian*, February 8, 2024, https://www.theguardian.com/commentisfree/2024/feb/08/iowa-anti-trans-bill-649.

6. John Fenaughty, Kyle Tan, Alex Ker, Jaimie Veale, Peter Saxton, and Mohamed Alansari, "Sexual Orientation and Gender Identity Change Efforts for Young People in New Zealand: Demographics, Types of Suggesters, and Associations with Mental Health," *Journal of Youth and Adolescence* 52, 149-164 (2023), https://doi.org/10.1007/s10964-022-01693-3.

7. Human Rights Campaign: Resources, "The Lies and Dangers of Efforts to Change Sexual Orientation or Gender Idenity," https://www.hrc.org/resources/the-lies-and-dangers-of-reparative-therapy.

8. Ibid.

9. Amanda Onion, "Stonewall Riots," History.com, published: May 31, 2017, last modified June 20, 2024, https://www.history.com/topics/gay-rights/the-stonewall-riots.

10. U.S. Department of Health & Human Services, "What Are HIV and AIDS?," HIV.gov., last modified: January 13, 2023, https://www.hiv.gov/hiv-basics/overview/about-hiv-and-aids/what-are-hiv-and-aids.

11. Joseph Bennington-Castro, Joseph, "How AIDS Remained an Unspoken—but Deadly—Epidemic for Years,"

History.com, published: June 1, 2020, last modified August 22, 2023, https://www.history.com/news/aids-epidemic-ronald-reagan.

12. Ibid.

13. Howard Markel, "Remembering Ryan White, the Teen Who Fought against the Stigma of AIDS," PBS NewsHour, April 8, 2016, https://www.pbs.org/newshour/health/remembering-ryan-white-the-teen-who-fought-against-the-stigma-of-aids.

14. American Red Cross, "Updated Eligibility Guidelines Make Way for a More Inclusive Donation Process," August 16, 2023, https://www.redcrossblood.org/local-homepage/news/article/inclusive-blood-donation-change-rcbs.html.

15. Centers for Disease Control and Prevention, "HIV-Specific Criminal Laws," December 19, 2019, https://www.cdc.gov/hiv/policies/law/states/exposure.html.

16. Ken Schneck and Rachel Dissell, "He's 23 and in an Ohio Prison for Exposing Someone to HIV—Even Though He Couldn't Transmit the Virus," *The Buckeye Flame*, March 13, 2024, https://thebuckeyeflame.com/2024/03/13/hes-23-and-in-an-ohio-prison/.

17. Centers for Disease Control and Prevention, "Let's Stop HIV Together: HIV Stigma," November 3, 2022, https://www.cdc.gov/stophivtogether/hiv-stigma/index.html#:~:text=Talking%20openly%20about%20HIV%20can.

18. National Alliance to End Homelessness, "State of Homelessness: 2023 Edition," https://endhomelessness.org/wp-content/uploads/2024/08/StateOfHomelessness_2023.pdf

19. National Coalition for the Homeless. "LGBTQ Homelessness." December 28, 2022. https://nationalhomelessness.org/lgbtq-homelessness.

20. Ibid.

21. Human Dignity Trust, "Map of Countries That Criminalise LGBT People," https://www.humandignitytrust.org/lgbt-the-law/map-of-criminalisation/.

22. Jacob Anderson-Minshall, "The Most Dangerous (and Safest) Places in the World for LGBTQ+ Travelers," *Out Traveler*, March 22, 2023, https://www.outtraveler.com/safety/dangerous-safest-countries-2023#rebelltitem13.

23. Annette Choi. "Record Number of Anti-LGBTQ Bills Were Introduced in 2023." CNN, January 3, 2024. https://www.cnn.com/politics/anti-lgbtq-plus-state-bill-rights-dg/index.html

24. Ken Schneck, "15 Quotes from the Third Hearing on HB 183 to Ban Trans Individuals from Bathrooms in Ohio Schools and Colleges," *The Buckeye Flame*, October 18, 2023, https://thebuckeyeflame.com/2023/10/18/15-quotes-from-the-third-hearing-on-hb-183/.

25. Ibid.

26. Advocates for Trans Equality, "Transgender People and Bathroom Access," https://transequality.org/issues/resources/transgender-people-and-bathroom-access.

27. OK S., SB129, Regular Sess., 2023, http://www.oklegislature.gov/BillInfo.aspx?Bill=SB129&session=2300.

28. FL S., S0254, Regular Sess., 2023, https://legiscan.com/FL/text/S0254/id/2799959.

29. The National LGBTQ+ Bar Association and Foundation, "LGBTQ+ 'Panic' Defense," https://lgbtqbar.org/programs/advocacy/gay-trans-panic-defense/.

30. Robert Black, "Wyo. Judge Bars 'Gay Panic' Defense," *Washington Post*, November 1, 1999. https://www.washingtonpost.com/wp-srv/national/daily/nov99/shepard110199.htm.

31. Julie Compton, "Alleged 'Gay Panic Defense' in Texas Murder Trial Stuns Advocates," NBC News, May 2, 2018. https://www.nbcnews.com/feature/nbc-out/alleged-gay-panic-defense-texas-murder-trial-stuns-advocates-n870571.

32. Movement Advancement Project, "Gay/Trans Panic Defense Bans," October 26, 2024, https://www.lgbtmap.org/equality-maps/panic_defense_bans.

3. LGBTQIA+ Around the World

1. Equaldex, "Explore the Progress of LGBTQ+ Rights across the World," Equaldex.com, October 26, 2024. https://www.equaldex.com/.

2. Danica Coto and Luis Andres Henao, "At a Glance: Laws in the Caribbean Region That Criminalize Gay Sex," *Associated Press*, June 11, 2023, https://apnews.com/article/lgbtq-caribbean-religion-antigay-law-christians-21b3bcf6fe6e8976109f-0c8e70050fd2.

3. Ibid.

4. Nicole Winfield, and David Crary, "Pope Approves Blessings for Same-Sex Couples That Must Not Resemble Marriage," *Associated Press*, December 18, 2023, https://apnews.com/article/vatican-lgbtq-pope-bfa5b71fa79055626e362936e739d1d8.

5. Delaney Ruth, "Central Ohio Catholics Respond to Pope's Shifting Same-Sex Policy," NBC4 WCMH-TV, December 19, 2023, https://www.nbc4i.com/news/local-news/columbus/central-ohio-catholics-respond-to-popes-shifting-same-sex-policy/.

6. Frederik Frandsen, "Hockey Is NOT for Everyone," Last Word on Sports, October 10, 2023. https://lastwordonsports.com/hockey/2023/10/10/hockey-is-not-for-everyone/.

4. Understanding and Supporting Gender Transitioning

1. William T. Houston, *Toxic Silence: Race, Black Gender Identity, and Addressing the Violence Against Black Transgender Women in Houston*, (New York: Peter Lang, 2018).

2. Keon West and Martha Lucia Borras-Guevara, "When Cisgender, Heterosexual Men Feel Attracted to Transgender Women: Sexuality-Norm Violations Lead to Compensatory Anti-Gay Prejudice," *Journal of Homosexuality* 69 (13) (2021):12267-2285. https://doi.org/10.1080/00918369.2021.1938467.

3. Cynthia Lee and Peter Kwan, "The Trans Panic Defense: Masculinity, Heteronormativity, and the Murder of Trans-

gender Women," 66 *Hastings Law Journal* 77 (2014), https://heinonline.org/HOL/LandingPage?handle=hein.journals/hastlj66&div=6&id=&page=.

4. Human Rights Campaign "Fatal Violence against the Transgender and Gender Expansive Community in 2022," https://www.hrc.org/resources/fatal-violence-against-the-transgender-and-gender-expansive-community-in-2022.

5. Sophia Cecelia Leveque, *Trans/Active: A Biography of Gwendolyn Ann Smith* (Winston-Salem, NC: Wake Forest University, Library Partners Press, 2017),

6. GenderGP, "Detransition Facts and Statistics 2021: Exploding the Myths around Detransitioning," July 5, 2024, https://www.gendergp.com/detransition-facts/.

7. Harry Barbee, Bashar Hassan and Fan Liang, "Transgender Regret? Research Challenges Narratives about Gender-Affirming Surgeries," The Conversation, January 22, 2024. https://theconversation.com/transgender-regret-research-challenges-narratives-about-gender-affirming-surgeries-220642.

7. Rebecca Minor, "'Passing' as Cisgender: Protection and Privilege," Gender Specialist, December 6, 2023, https://www.genderspecialist.com/blog/passing-as-cisgender.

8. TransHub, "Passing," https://www.transhub.org.au/passing.

9. Pratyush, Dayal, "How Beauty Standards for LGBTQ People Impact Body Image, Mental Health," CBC, September 29, 2022, https://www.cbc.ca/news/canada/saskatoon/beauty-standards-lgbtq-body-image-mental-health-1.6591806.

10. Alok Vaid-Menon, "We Shouldn't Have to Pass in Order to Be Safe," September 17, 2014, https://www.alokvmenon.com/blog/2017/3/12/we-shouldnt-have-to-pass-in-order-to-be-safe.

11. them, "What Does It Mean to Be Intersex?," July 15, 2022, https://www.them.us/story/inqueery-intersex.

12. Cleveland Clinic, "Intersex: What Is Intersex, Gender Identity, Intersex Surgery," July 19, 2022, https://

my.clevelandclinic.org/health/articles/16324-intersex.

13. Global Intersex Inclusive Pride Flag, "The Home of the Global Inclusive Pride Flag Project," https://www.globalinclusiveprideflag.com/.

14. Jason Rafferty, "Gender Identity Development in Children," HealthyChildren.org, May 11, 2022, https://www.healthychildren.org/English/ages-stages/gradeschool/Pages/Gender-Identity-and-Gender-Confusion-In-Children.aspx#:~:text=Gender%20identity%20typically%20develops%20in.

15. Ibid.

16. Advocates for Trans Equality, "Get the Facts: The Truth about Transition-Related Care for Transgender Youth," National Center for Transgender Equality, February 28, 2023, https://transequality.org/blog/get-the-facts-the-truth-about-transition-related-care-for-transgender-youth.

17. U.S. Dept of Health and Human Services, Office of Population Affairs, "Gender-Affirming Care and Young People," https://opa.hhs.gov/sites/default/files/2022-03/gender-affirming-care-young-people-march-2022.pdf.

18. The Trevor Project, "Gender-Affirming Care for Youth," https://www.thetrevorproject.org/research-briefs/gender-affirming-care-for-youth/.

19. Mayo Clinic Staff, "Pubertal Blockers for Transgender and Gender Diverse Youth," Mayo Clinic, June 14, 2023. https://www.mayoclinic.org/diseases-conditions/gender-dysphoria/in-depth/pubertal-blockers/art-20459075.

20. Chase Strangio and Gabriel Arkles, "Four Myths about Trans Athletes, Debunked," American Civil Liberties Union, April 30, 2020, https://www.aclu.org/news/lgbtq-rights/four-myths-about-trans-athletes-debunked.

21. Ibid.

22. Tony Morrison, "FACT CHECK: Olympic Boxer Imane Khelif, Participation and Eligibility of Paris 2024," GLAAD, August 2, 2024, https://glaad.org/fact-check-partic-

ipation-and-eligibility-of-paris-2024-olympic-boxers-imane-khelif-and-lin-yu-ting/.

23. Children's Hospital Colorado, "X&Y Chromosome Variations,"https://www.childrenscolorado.org/conditions-and-advice/conditions-and-symptoms/conditions/x-y-chromo-some-variations/.

24. Gender Justice, "Get the Facts: Trans Equity in Sports," https://www.genderjustice.us/get-the-facts-trans-equity-in-sports/.

5. Gender-Affirming Medical Care

1. Aetna, "Gender Affirming Surgery," Medical Clinical Policy Bulletin, No. 0615, last review as of December 102, 2024, https://www.aetna.com/cpb/medical/data/600_699/0615.html.

2. Metro Health, "Transgender & Non-Binary Care FAQ," https://www.metrohealth.org/lgbtq-pride-network/adult-transgender-non-binary-care/transgender-non-binary-care-faq.

3. GenderGP, "Survey Shines a Light on NHS Trans Experiences," https://www.gendergp.com/survey-shows-trans-lack-trust-nhs/.

4. Lindsey Dawson and Jennifer Kates, "The Proliferation of State Actions Limiting Youth Access to Gender Affirming Care," KFF, January 31, 2024, https://www.kff.org/policy-watch/the-proliferation-of-state-actions-limiting-youth-access-to-gender-affirming-care/.

5. P. Grootens-Wiegers, "Targeted Informed Consent: Empowering Young Participants in Medical-Scientific Research," Scholarly Publications Leiden University, December 2016, https://scholarlypublications.universiteitleiden.nl/access/item%3A2893591/download.

6. Office of Population Affairs, "Gender-Affirming Care and Young People." https://ia601409.us.archive.org/22/items/office-of-population-affairs-gender-affirming-care-young-people-march-2022/OFFICE%20OF%20POPULATION%20

AFFAIRS%20-%20gender-affirming-care-young-people-march-2022.pdf

7. Ibid.

6. Understanding Sexuality

1. International Planned Parenthood Federation, "Resource: From Evidence to Action: Advocating for Comprehensive Sexuality Education," https://www.ippf.org/resource/evidence-action-advocating-comprehensive-sexuality-education.

2. The American College of Obstetricians and Gynecologists, "Comprehensive Sexuality Education," https://www.acog.org/clinical/clinical-guidance/committee-opinion/articles/2016/11/comprehensive-sexuality-education#:~:text=Studies%20have%20demonstrated%20that%20comprehensive.

3. Ibid.

7. Pronouns and Lived Names

1. Miriam Berger, "A Guide to How Gender-Neutral Language Is Developing around the World," *Washington Post*, December 15, 2019, https://www.washingtonpost.com/world/2019/12/15/guide-how-gender-neutral-language-is-developing-around-world/.

2. Wren Sanders, "How to Affirm the People in Your Life Who Use Multiple Sets of Pronouns," them, March 5, 2021, https://www.them.us/story/multiple-sets-of-pronouns.

3. Len Meyer, "Why Are Pronouns so Important?" Planned Parenthood of Illinois, Blog, June 30, 2021, https://www.plannedparenthood.org/planned-parenthood-illinois/blog/why-are-pronouns-so-important-2.

4. Serin Bond-Yancey, "Beyond Inclusion: Pronoun Use for Health and Well-Being," Community Commosn, https://communitycommons.org/collections/Pronouns-and-Well-Being

8. Responding To Anti-LGBTQIA+ Rhetoric and Attitudes

1. Wendy D. Manning, Marshal Neal Fettro, and Esther Lamidi, "Child Well-Being in Same-Sex Parent Families: Review of Research Prepared for American Sociological Association Amicus Brief," *Population Research and Policy Review* 33 (4): 485–502, https://doi.org/10.1007/s11113-014-9329-6.

2. GLAAD, "Transgenderism: Definition, Meaning, and Origin in Anti-LGBTQ Hate," https://glaad.org/transgenderism-definition-meaning-anti-lgbt-online-hate/.

3. Robyn Ochs, (@robynochs). 2021. "I call myself bisexual because I acknowledge that I have in myself the potential to be attracted," X, July, 13, 2021, 4:33pm, https://x.com/robynochs/status/1415046733923590144?lang=en

4. Williams Institute, UCLA School of Law, "Press Release: LGBT People Nearly Four Times More Likely than Non-LGBT People to Be Victims of Violent Crime," October 2, 2020, https://williamsinstitute.law.ucla.edu/press/ncvs-lgbt-violence-press-release/.

5. Autism Research Institute, "LGBTQIA+ and Autism," https://autism.org/lgbtq-and-autism/.

6. Chelsea Koutroulis, "Understanding the Difference between Kink and Fetish: Exploring Therapy Options," Oaks Counseling Associates, Resources, June 12, 2023, https://oakscounselingassociates.com/understanding-the-difference-between-a-kink-and-a-fetish-exploring-therapy-options/.

7. American Civil Liberties Union, "Mapping Attacks on LGBTQ Rights in U.S. State Legislatures in 2024," https://www.aclu.org/legislative-attacks-on-lgbtq-rights-2024.

9. Intersecctionality and Creating Safe Spaces

1. Darcie Shinberger, "LGBTQI* & Intersectionality: Going Beyond Pride Month," National Alliance on Mental Illness, June 12, 2023, https://namiillinois.org/lgbtqi-intersectionality-going-beyond-pride-month/

2. Victoria Nguyen, "Amplifying Marginalized Voices: Why It Matters," David Eccles School of Business, March 29, 2022,

https://eccles.utah.edu/news/amplifying-marginalized-voices-why-it-matters/.

3. Ibid.

4. Kerith J. Conron, "LGBT Youth Population in the United States," Williams Institute, UCLA School of Law, September 2020, https://williamsinstitute.law.ucla.edu/wp-content/uploads/LGBT-Youth-US-Pop-Sep-2020.pdf.

5. Drexel University School of Education, "The Importance of Multicultural Education," https://drexel.edu/soe/resources/student-teaching/advice/importance-of-cultural-diversity-in-classroom/#:~:text=Naturally%2C%20by%20exposing%20students%20to.

6. Laura Meckler, Hannah Natanson, and John Harden, "In States with Laws Targeting LGBTQ Issues, School Hate Crimes Quadrupled," *Washington Post*, March 12, 2024, https://www.washingtonpost.com/education/2024/03/12/school-lgbtq-hate-crimes-incidents/.

7. Human Rights Campaign, "LGBTQ Youth in the Foster Care System," https://www.thehrcfoundation.org/professional-resources/lgbtq-youth-in-the-foster-care-system.

8. Ibid.

9. Movement Advancement Project, "Equality Maps: Child Welfare Nondiscrimination Laws," https://www.lgbtmap.org/equality-maps/foster_and_adoption_laws.

10. Youth.Gov, "Youth Topics: Child Welfare," Interagency Working Group on Youth Programs, https://youth.gov/youth-topics/lgbtq-youth/child-welfare#_ftn.

11. Caroline Medina and Lindsay Mahowald, "Discrimination and Barriers to Well-Being: The State of the LGBTQI+ Community in 2022," Center for American Progress, January 12, 2023, https://www.americanprogress.org/article/discrimination-and-barriers-to-well-being-the-state-of-the-lgbtqi-community-in-2022/.

12. Lucy Thackray, "Virgin Atlantic Job Applications Double after Gendered Uniforms Scrapped," *The Independent*,

November 3, 2022, https://www.independent.co.uk/travel/news-and-advice/virgin-atlantic-dress-code-job-applications-double-b2216703.html.

13. Superscript, "14 Ways to Create an LGBTQ+ Inclusive Workplace in 2023," June 17, 2024, https://gosuperscript.com/news-and-resources/how-to-create-an-lgbt-inclusive-workplace/.

14. "We Help Leaders Build Inclusive Culture at Scale," The Diversity Movement,https://thediversitymovement.com/.

15. Lacie Blankenship, "5 Tips for Managing an LGBTQ+ Inclusive Workplace," Vanderbilt Business School, June 17, 2022, https://business.vanderbilt.edu/news/2022/06/17/5-tips-for-managing-an-lgbtq-inclusive-workplace/.

10. Being An Ally To Someone Who Is Coming Out

1. GLAAD, "Guide to Anti-LGBTQ Online Hate and Disinformation," June 12, 2023, https://glaad.org/smsi/anti-lgbtq-online-hate-speech-disinformation-guide/.

11. Religion and the LGBTQIA+ Community

1. LOVEboldy, "About Us | Loveboldly," https://www.love-boldly.net/about-us.

2. Amy Aspey, in discussion with the author regarding Christianity and the LGBTQIA+ Community,

3. Sarah Pruitt, "Why the King James Bible of 1611 Remains the Most Popular Translation in History, " History.com, April 16, 2019, https://www.history.com/news/king-james-bible-most-popular.

4. Abraham Smith, "NRSV Updated Edition," Perspective Online, January 4, 2022, https://blog.smu.edu/perkins/nrsv-updated-edition/.

5. Queer Bible Hermeneutics, "Lost in Translation: Alternative Meaning in Leviticus 18:22," Perkins School of Theology, April 11, 2019, https://blog.smu.edu/ot8317/2019/04/11/lost-in-translation-alternative-meaning-in-leviticus-1822/

6. The Reformation Project, "Brief Biblical Case for LGBTQ Inclusion: 9. 1 Corinthians and 1 Timothy Address Exploitation," https://reformationproject.org/case/1-corinthians-and-1-timothy/.

7. "1946: The Mistranslation That Shifted a Culture." 1https://www.1946themovie.com/.

8. Aspey, interview with the author.

9. Aspey, interview with the author.

10. Robertson-Wesley United Church, "Affirming Theology —the Genderqueer Adam," January 30, 2020. https://www.rwuc.org/2020/01/30/affirming-theology-the-genderqueer-adam/.

11. Aspey, interview with the author.

12. Aspey, interview with the author.

13. Aspey, interview with the author.

14. Ari Jun, interview with the author,

15. Umi Sumbulah, "Ibn Arabi's Thought on Wahdat Al-Wujud and Its Relevance to Religious Diversity," *Ulumuna* 20 (1): 29–50, https://doi.org/10.20414/ujis.v20i1.793.

16. Noel Rae, "How Christian Slaveholders Used the Bible to Justify Slavery," *Time*, February 23, 2018. https://time.com/5171819/christianity-slavery-book-excerpt/.

www.ingramcontent.com/pod-product-compliance
Lightning Source LLC
Jackson TN
JSHW020301170225
79125JS00002B/3